The Making of
an Adult Educator

The Making of
an Adult Educator

An Autobiographical Journey

Malcolm S. Knowles

Foreword by
Leonard Nadler and Zeace Nadler

THE MAKING OF AN ADULT EDUCATOR
An Autobiographical Journey
  by Malcolm S. Knowles

Copyright © 1989 by: Jossey-Bass Inc., Publishers
                    350 Sansome Street
                    San Francisco, California 94104
                              &
                    Jossey-Bass Limited
                    28 Banner Street
                    London EC1Y 8QE

Library of Congress Cataloging-in-Publication Data

Knowles, Malcolm Shepherd, date.
    The making of an adult educator: an autobiographical journey /
Malcolm S. Knowles : foreword by Leonard Nadler and Zeace Nadler.
        p.   cm. — (Jossey-Bass higher education series) (Jossey-Bass
management series)
        Bibliography: p.
        Includes index.
        ISBN 1-55542-169-5
        1. Knowles, Malcolm Shepherd, date.   2. Adult education
teachers—United States—Biography.   3. Adult education—United
States.   I. Title.   II. Series.   III. Series: Jossey-Bass
management series.
LA2317.K567A3   1989
374'.92—dc20
[B]   89-11121
                                                         CIP

Manufactured in the United States of America

The paper in this book meets the guidelines for
permanence and durability of the Committee on
Production Guidelines for Book Longevity of the
Council on Library Resources.

JACKET DESIGN BY WILLI BAUM

FIRST EDITION

Code 8943

A joint publication in
The Jossey-Bass
Higher Education Series
and
The Jossey-Bass
Management Series

Consulting Editors
Human Resources

Leonard Nadler
Zeace Nadler
College Park, Maryland

Contents

Foreword

The Making of an Adult Educator provides a rare opportunity to meet Malcolm S. Knowles, whose impact on the field of adult learning has been and will continue to be outstanding. Only rarely do we have the privilege of sharing the inner thoughts of a leader while that person is still alive and measuring those thoughts against performance.

Malcolm is an authentic person; what you read is what he is. If you have had the opportunity to work with him, you know that he not only espouses concepts of adults as learners but that he also practices them.

When Malcolm invited us to write this foreword, our first reaction was great pleasure. Then, we thought that we should suggest other people who deserved that honor. However, when Malcolm's editor at Jossey-Bass reinforced his request, we reexamined our decision. After all, we have known Malcolm and his wife, Hulda, for more than thirty years, professionally and personally, and have liked, respected, and greatly admired him—so why not us?

We had, of course, read his manuscript. We learned much about Malcolm that we and surely others had not previously known, which is why we thought this book was such an important contribution. In a sense, we "get into the head" of an international leader in the field of adult learning. We find, for example, that he does not remain stagnant. He does not develop a point of view and then set it in concrete.

This is important, for one of his major contributions is to challenge all of us in the field of adult learning to examine our concepts and assumptions about adults as learners. Probably the outstanding example is his development of the concept of andragogy. As might be expected, some practitioners and professors picked up the basic ideas and attempted to apply them to all situations of adult learning. This was undoubtedly due in part to Malcolm's early work on the concept, as he wrote of "andragogy *versus* pedagogy." After discussion, feedback, and practice, however, Malcolm now writes of "andragogy *and* pedagogy." This is just one of several developments in Malcolm's thinking that is obvious when one reads this book.

His contributions go far beyond his writings and teaching. In thinking about this foreword, we realized that we might show some other dimensions of Malcolm and how he has influenced the field.

One incident occurred in 1958, when Malcolm was the executive director of the Adult Education Association (AEA). A group of eight of us got together at the IBM Club in Binghamton, New York, to explore how we could bring together the AEA and the American Society for Training and Development (ASTD). At that time, the AEA had three times as many members as the ASTD, but there was an obvious overlap in membership and purpose. Leaders from both organizations (volunteers and staff) were in Binghamton.

Although the meeting did not have a positive outcome, it was the first time that some of us had an opportunity to really see Malcolm in action with a group. He not only taught and wrote about group process—he practiced it. It was a very rewarding professional experience, despite our inability to achieve our goal. We all came away from the session with glowing words of praise for the way in which Malcolm had functioned in both a process and a content role.

Readers of *The Making of an Adult Educator* will gain a significant understanding of Malcolm as he shares with us his insight into those who helped him develop. Some of it may sound like a litany of leaders, but Malcolm was privileged to know them and to learn from them. In this book, he tells us how some of that learning took place. In his usual modest fashion, however, he does not relate how he helped other leaders in the field in their own professional growth.

There is one incident we must share, and it involves our students and Malcolm's wife, Hulda. For many years we had conducted a class from George Washington University at the annual ASTD conference. Our students, almost all graduates and from several universities, would meet with us each day of the conference to process the learning for that day. We would invite professionals of stature to come to class for about half an hour. The purpose was to enable our students to meet some of the leaders in the field in a less formal situation than a session and to provide those leaders with some direct contact with people who would in turn probably be future human resource development leaders.

At one conference, we invited Malcolm. Despite his very busy schedule (everybody wants to meet with Malcolm, and he has difficulty turning anybody down), he agreed to come to one of our half-hour sessions. When he arrived, the students sat in awe and just waited for him to pontificate. Of course, that does not happen with Malcolm! It took just a few minutes for him to get them involved. Suddenly, it was an hour later. We called for a break to give Malcolm a chance to leave. During the break, he continued to make himself available to the students and then asked us if he could come back to the class for another hour. Naturally, we readily concurred.

That evening, we were seated with Hulda at a table at a function where Malcolm was receiving an award. We related the incident to Hulda and shared with her the reaction of our students. They stated to us that they felt that they had been in the presence of a real leader—a person who was so far above others that in one sense he was up in the clouds—and yet what he had to share was down-to-earth. Hulda looked at us and said in surprise, "But, he is only Malcolm!"

Quite an understatement. Yet it discloses the humility and humanity that epitomize both Malcolm and Hulda Knowles.

You will enjoy reading *The Making of an Adult Educator;* but, even more, you will get to know a man who has provided significant leadership to the field of adult learning.

College Park, Maryland   Leonard Nadler
July 1989   Zeace Nadler

Preface

I have had more fun writing *The Making of an Adult Educator* than any book I have written before. Here is why: About two years ago my editor at Jossey-Bass said to me, "Malcolm, we have never asked one of our authors to do this before, but in your case we'd like you to write a series of essays—short, medium, or long—in which you say things you have wanted to say but haven't said yet or would say differently from what you have said before." This sounded like such a challenging opportunity that I agreed at once.

I thought for a while about what I have wanted to say but have not yet said, and what came into my mind were highly personal experiences that influenced the shaping of my life. My previous books had all been organized around concepts, theories, principles, and methods, framed within a logical outline. I cited personal experiences when they fit into the outline and illuminated some abstraction, but they were more illustrative than substantive.

So I sat down at my computer and started reminiscing about things that had happened to me that I learned from and that caused me to become what I have become: a committed professional adult educator. My fingers started flying as I let them flow with the sparks set off by my neurons. I felt a sense of freedom that I had never before experienced in writing; I was not boxed into a predetermined logical structure.

Overview of the Contents

What began taking shape was a sort of autobiography, but only sort of. There emerged a series of episodes that seemed more or less isolated as I recalled them but that gradually, with some rearrangement, became loosely connected. So what I ended up with is a series of snapshots of a life in the process of becoming something: in this case, an adult educator. I originally gave the manuscript the working title *The Making of an Adult Educator.* But when I started sharing this title with friends, I got the reaction "great—a manual on how to become an adult educator." I protested that it was not a how-to-do-it manual but rather the story of how *I* became an adult educator. Sure, I would explain, I hope that it might contain some insights and tips that would be useful to people in the field or to people considering entering the field, but it is self-revelatory rather than prescriptive in its intent. It was at that point that I decided I had better add the subtitle, *An Autobiographical Journey.*

Chapter One describes the people and forces that have influenced me, from boyhood until now. It provides a kind of broad-stroke overview of a life-span developmental process that is further illuminated by episodes described in later chapters. This chapter is the closest thing to a sequential autobiographical essay in the book.

Chapter Two portrays eight particularly impactive episodes that deepened my insights, skills, or competencies in certain areas of my life.

Chapter Three recaptures the landmark episodes and highlights the individual "heroes" who influenced my understanding of the history of adult education in this country.

Chapter Four attempts to trace the evolution of my thinking about adult learning, with special attention to crucial turning points in that evolutionary process.

Chapter Five identifies fifteen questions I am most frequently asked in workshops, conferences, and courses and describes the answers I give to those questions. This chapter provides a vehicle for me to deal with a variety of miscellaneous issues that do not fit neatly into other chapters.

Chapter Six describes how I am evaluated in my workshops and courses, in personal correspondence, and in the literature and shows how I react to these evaluations. This chapter demonstrates how systematic evaluation has been one of the chief sources of energy for both my personal and professional growth.

Chapter Seven describes my experiences trying to exploit the new technologies of education, especially the electronic media. I make some predictions about the potential for these technologies in future systems for delivering educational resources to learners at their convenience in terms of time, place, and pace.

Chapter Eight presents my fantasies about the future of education, which challenges me to think about how people should be educated to survive—if not excel—in the twenty-first century. This chapter provides a vehicle for me to express some ideas about how our entire educational enterprise might be reorganized around the concept of lifelong self-directed learning. The second section of this chapter comes close to being a prescription for becoming an adult educator, identifying the competencies I believe are involved in performing that role in contemporary society. This section also projects my optimistic view of the future of careers in adult education.

The last chapter lists the articles I have written and gives brief explanations of what they are about and why I wrote them. It provides documentary evidence of the changes that have taken place in my interests and thinking.

Acknowledgments

Many people deserve thanks for bringing *The Making of an Adult Educator* into being. Most noteworthy, of course, are the scores of people mentioned in the book who have contributed to my career. More immediately, I want to thank my editor, Lynn Luckow, my consulting editors, Leonard and Zeace Nadler, and three anonymous reviewers for both their encouragement to write the book and their many helpful suggestions for making it better. Most thanks of all goes to my wife, Hulda, for enduring the hours of solitude while

I was at work in my study, for reading the manuscript for coherence and accuracy, and for insisting on honesty.

I wrote this book primarily because it was fun to write. But I hope it provides some information, insights, and hope that will be helpful to people who are considering or have already chosen a career in adult education. Most of all, I hope that *The Making of an Adult Educator* will be as much fun to read as it was to write.

Raleigh, North Carolina   Malcolm S. Knowles
July 1989

The Author

Malcolm S. Knowles is professor emeritus of adult and community college education at North Carolina State University and previously was professor of education at Boston University, executive director of the Adult Education Association of the U.S.A., and director of adult education at the YMCAs in Boston, Detroit, and Chicago. He received his B.A. degree (1934) from Harvard College and his M.A. degree (1949) and his Ph.D. degree (1960) from the University of Chicago—all in education. He has honorary degrees from Lowell Technical Institute, the National College of Education, and Regis College.

Knowles's main academic and professional interests have been in the theory and practice of adult education. In addition to administering adult education programs and teaching in graduate schools, he has done consulting and conducted workshops for a wide variety of organizations and corporations in North America, Europe, South America, and Australia. His books include *Informal Adult Education* (1950), *Teaching Adults in Informal Courses* (1954), *How to Develop Better Leaders* (with Hulda Knowles, 1955), *Introduction to Group Dynamics* (with Hulda Knowles, 1959; rev. ed., 1972), *Handbook of Adult Education in the U.S.* (editor, 1962), *The Adult Education Movement in the United States* (1962; rev. ed., 1977), *Higher Adult Education in the United States* (1969), *The*

Modern Practice of Adult Education: From Pedagogy to Andragogy (1970; rev. ed., 1980), *The Adult Learner: A Neglected Species* (1973; rev. ed., 1984), *Self-Directed Learning: A Guide for Learners and Teachers* (1975), *Andragogy in Action: Applying Modern Principles of Adult Learning* (with others, 1984), and *Using Learning Contracts: Practical Approaches to Individualizing and Structuring Learning* (1986).

During his retirement, Knowles is serving as a mentor for the Fielding Institute's external degree program in human and organizational development, as national lecturer for the Nova University Center for Higher Education, as adjunct professor of the Union Graduate School, and as a member of the Task Force on Lifelong Education of the UNESCO Institute for Education, for which he has written a chapter, "Creating Lifelong Learning Communities," for its forthcoming book on lifelong education.

The Making of
an Adult Educator

Chapter 1

Becoming an Adult Educator:
My Journey

I started this chapter with the title "People I Wish I Had Been Able to Thank" because over the years I have thought about the many people who made significant contributions to my personal development whom I have not thanked for what they did for me. I changed the title to "People I Have Learned From" when I realized that the central dynamic of their contributions is that I learned from them. I would like to thank them now by sharing them with you and revealing in the process how I became what I am. Then, about halfway through writing this chapter, I realized that what it is really about is the making of an adult educator, for in looking back on my career, it seems so well planned and in such a straight line toward a preconceived goal. That isn't the way it was at all. I was just exposed by happenstance to people and events that helped me move in that direction.

The Early Years

I want to start with my father, Dr. Albert D. Knowles. He was a veterinarian in Missoula, Montana. From the time I was about four years old, he took me with him on his visits to farms and ranches to treat sick or injured animals. While driving to and from these locations, we engaged in serious discussions about all sorts of subjects, such as the meaning of life, right and wrong, religion, politics, success, happiness,

1

and everything else a growing child is curious about. I distinctly remember feeling like a companion rather than an inferior. My father often asked me what I thought before he said what he thought, and he gave me the feeling that he respected my mind. When he was operating on an animal, I would help by holding instruments and he would explain what he was doing and why. I still remember a lot about the anatomy of cows and horses. Even after I started school, I would take trips with him after school and on weekends. Probably the most significant learning I gained from interaction with my father was a positive self-concept, self-respect. But I also learned a good deal about the importance of values, especially honesty, generosity, integrity, fairness, and authenticity. I learned something, too, about how to think critically and how to learn from other people by asking good questions.

An incident that occurred in 1937 burned the impression of my father's character into my soul. I was the director of training for the National Youth Administration of Massachusetts and was attending a meeting of the National Advisory Council for the NYA in Washington. I was introduced to one of its distinguished members, Mary McLeod Bethune, founder of the Bethune-Cookman College for black students in Daytona Beach, Florida. When she heard my name, she asked, "Are you any relation to Dr. Albert Knowles, the veterinarian in West Palm Beach?" I said he was my father, and she threw her arms around me and hugged me, saying, "I am so glad to meet the son of the most humane veterinarian in Florida. He is the only one I know who will treat my people's pets, and doesn't charge them if they can't afford to pay."

My learnings from my mother were, I think, less cognitive and more affective. And they were conveyed more by her example than by inquiry. The extent to which I am a tender, loving, caring person I owe largely to her. She also reinforced my self-concept as being an OK person. I remember, for example, that when I was fifteen and debating whether or not to apply for admission to Harvard, she said, "Why not? You're just as good as if not better than any other students who are applying."

Then there was Miss Utley, my fourth-grade teacher at Roosevelt Grammar School in Missoula. After a month or so of our studying arithmetic she gave us a test. The next morning she announced that she had scored the test and had an important piece of news. She held up one of the test papers (I thought it looked like mine) and said something like, "For the first time since I have been giving this test, I have received an absolutely perfect answer sheet. We are fortunate to have such an able student in our class—Malcolm Knowles." She asked me to come up to the front of class to get my paper and a pat on the back while my fellow fourth-graders applauded. Until that event I had thought of myself as just another boy; an OK boy, but nothing special. From that time on, though, I thought of myself as a smart boy. And I have been smart ever since. Thank you, Miss Utley.

This positive self-concept was reinforced by Mr. Sargeant, principal of the Kelsey City (now Palm Beach Gardens), Florida, elementary school. My family had moved from Missoula to Kelsey City in 1925, and I enrolled in the sixth grade in Mr. Sargeant's school, where he also taught the combined sixth and seventh grades. Within weeks it became clear that I was doing the seventh-grade assignments, and he called me into his office and told me that he was promoting me to the seventh grade, skipping the sixth grade. He gave me the impression that it was because I was so smart; it wasn't until much later that I realized that the real reason probably was that the school in Missoula was more advanced than the one in Kelsey City.

During the next several years I was active in the Boy Scouts under the leadership of Reverend Pusey, our scoutmaster. It was here that I learned the meaning of ambition and that I could achieve anything I was really committed to. As described in the next chapter, I earned fifty merit badges, won a free trip to the world jamboree in England, and wrote my first published article describing my system for achieving the most that could possibly be achieved in a given length of time. I also became a patrol leader and the troop leader under Reverend Pusey's tutelage, and our troop won several awards for outstanding achievements. Actually, I have found that the knowledge and skills I gained in the process of learning the content of over fifty merit badges and performing a leadership role were as important in my development as everything I learned in my high school courses.

But one pair of high school courses stand out as a highlight—the two courses in English composition I took as a sophomore and junior with Miss Anderson. Instead of having us memorize rules of grammar, sentence structure, punctuation, and the like, which I had expected, she had us start right out writing short essays (the first one, I remember, was the story of our life to date), then critiquing them in groups of three and extracting principles of composition from this analysis. Miss Anderson, of course, raised questions about any unsubstantiated findings. It was through this experience that I began to get the feeling that I might be able to be a writer and that I enjoyed writing. She made writing fun rather than drudgery. I demonstrated my newly developed skills and excitement by writing a newspaper column and the award-winning editorial described in Chapter Two. I might add that all of my high school teachers gave me the impression that I was an able student (I was the valedictorian of my class), which encouraged me to apply for a Rhodes scholarship and admission to Harvard College in my senior year. I won the regional competition for the Rhodes scholarship but lost out in the national finals (a side trip I now don't regret) and was accepted, with a scholarship, at Harvard. (I suspect that Harvard didn't have many applicants from the Southeast during those Depression years.)

My experience at Harvard was generally enriching, but one teacher stands out especially in my memory. He was Alfred North Whitehead, a visiting lecturer from England in my junior year. I learned from him that a lecture can be an exciting adventure in inquiry. He started the opening session by saying, "Gentlemen, this is listed as a course in philosophy. It is not. It is a course in philosophizing. Who has a philosophical issue you'd like to explore?" One of the two hundred students present shouted out, "Truth." "A very good issue," Whitehead said, and proceeded to think aloud with us for over an hour about the possible meanings of truth. We students were sitting on the edge of our seats thinking with him, not taking notes for an exam. Of course, the other courses I took at Harvard—in literature, history, political science, ethics, and international law—broadened my intellectual perspective and no doubt taught me something about critical thinking. But my extracurricular activities as president of the Harvard Liberal Club, general secretary of the New England Model League of Nations, and president of the Phillips Brooks House contributed every bit as much to my development as a person.

A couple of nonacademic people also influenced my development while I was at Harvard. One was John Kingman, director of youth programs at Lincoln House, a settlement house in Boston. I had decided to give one evening a week of volunteer service to Phillips Brooks House, Harvard's social service agency, and in my sophomore year was referred to Mr. Kingman. The opening he had at the time was for an adviser of a club of early adolescent boys, and I suggested that my prior experience with the Boy Scouts qualified me. He explained that these boys were not exactly Boy Scout types and proceeded to give me a private tutorial on the sociology of poverty. But he emphasized that they were basically good kids who could make something of themselves if given the right guidance and support. I worked with this group for three years, with Mr. Kingman helping me through weekly consultations to plan and carry out activities with them. I think I learned more about human motivation and self-actualization from this experience than I could have learned from any number of courses. Members of my group won many prizes while I was their adviser—in sports, arts and crafts, dramatics, and community service. All but one finished high school, and several went on to college. What I later came to perceive as my deep faith in people got a strong impetus from my exposure to Mr. Kingman.

The other person who influenced me was Edward R. Murrow. At the beginning of my junior year, an announcement appeared in the *Harvard Crimson* that the Institute of International Education would give a scholarship to one Harvard student for a summer of study at its headquarters in Geneva, Switzerland. The basis of selection would be an essay titled "The Challenge and Promise of the League of Nations" and an interview with Edward R. Murrow, chairman of the selection committee. I decided that I would be the one to go to Geneva and spent many hours in the library finding out all I could about the League of Nations. I wrote and submitted my essay and about a month later received a notice of a time and place for my interview with Murrow. He opened the interview by complimenting me on my essay and then asked me a series of questions about who I was as a person, what my value system was, how I analyzed the world situation, what my aspirations were. I got the impression that Murrow's decision about the selection would be based more on my quality as a person than on the quality of my essay. He recommended me, and I spent the next summer in Geneva, seeing the League of Nations in action and talking with delegates from many nations. I corresponded with Murrow for almost a year about my experience and the issues it was eliciting. He responded with the warmth of an old friend; talk about a quality person! Concern for the quality of people over the quality of their products has been a theme in my life ever since.

Launching My Career

As a result of this experience, I decided to make my career in the U.S. Foreign Service. After I graduated from Harvard in 1934, I enrolled in the Fletcher School of Law and Diplomacy, sponsored jointly by Harvard and Tufts universities, and I took the Foreign Service exam. I was notified by the State Department that I had passed the exam but that the department was filling only the most urgent vacancies— and those were being filled by people who had passed the exam in 1932; so there would be at least a three-year wait. I had been married in August 1935 and needed a job to support a wife. A few days after I received the notice from the

State Department, there appeared in the *Boston Globe* an announcement that the federal government was establishing the National Youth Administration as a work-study program for unemployed youth between the ages of eighteen and twenty-five and that the state director for Massachusetts was Eddie Casey, former football coach at Harvard. I had got to know Eddie when I was a water boy for the Harvard football team—a way to get into the games free. I called Eddie and reminded him of my water-boy days and said I needed a job. He invited me to come to talk with his deputy, Bill Stern. Bill explained to me that there was just one position on the state staff that had not already been filled by a political appointment—the director of "related training," the half of the program designed to help make youth more employable. He also explained that the legislation establishing the NYA specified that each state staff must include at least one youth between eighteen and twenty-five and that he was having a tough time finding someone that age who knew anything about training. When he asked me if I knew anything about training, I replied, "Oh, yes," and described my experience as the adviser of a boys' club at Lincoln House while at Harvard. He pronounced me qualified. I am certain that my main qualification was my age, but I learned from Bill Stern that experience may be more important in employment situations than academic qualifications.

My responsibility consisted of finding out what skills employers were looking for, finding instructors to teach those skills, finding locations for courses to meet in, and recruiting youth to take the courses. I immediately formed an advisory council and began finding some direction. At that time there were no publications in the field that I knew about to tell me how to go about doing my job. But one of the members of the advisory council, Dorothy Hewitt, gave me a copy of a book she had written with Kirtley Mather, *Adult Education: A Dynamic for Democracy* (1937), describing how they had gone about organizing and marketing the Boston Center for Adult Education. It provided me with the practical guidelines I needed.

I met my first real mentor, Eduard C. Lindeman, about three months after becoming the director of related training for the NYA. Lindeman had just become director of training and recreation projects for the Works Progress Administration, and one of his responsibilities was supervising the training operations of the NYA in the various states. Soon after starting my job in Massachusetts, I got a call from Lindeman inviting me to have dinner with him, an event that was repeated several times a year for the next several years; he preferred to do business in a comfortable setting. We discussed my plans for launching a program of courses to improve the employability of the unemployed youth. The thing I remember most vividly about this first encounter was the intensity with which Lindeman listened to me; his facial expression and eyes were a classic study in concentration.

In subsequent meetings, I engaged with him in a mutual exploration of the meaning of adult education, its broad social aims, the unique characteristics of adults as learners, and the methods of learning most effective with them. With his gentle and subtle guidance, I conducted needs assessments, organized courses around life tasks, hired instructors who were proficient practitioners rather than academicians, conducted in-service training programs on the use of experiential methods, and in many other ways had a great adventure in exploring the strange new world of adult education.

I had heard people talk about Lindeman's *The Meaning of Adult Education,* published in 1926, but I was unable to get a copy; it was out of print. One day I mentioned this to Lindeman, and the next time we met he presented me with a copy that he had retrieved from the widow of a former student. I was so excited in reading it that I couldn't put it down. It became my chief source of inspiration and ideas for a quarter of a century. I still reread it at least once a year for the inspiration of seeing ideas and insights that were formulated before 1926 but have only in recent times been validated by research. I regard Lindeman as the prophet of modern adult educational theory.

In 1937 I was attending a meeting at which I was introduced to someone who asked me what I was doing. When I told him about my job at the NYA, he said, "Oh, you're an adult educator." I replied, "I am?" and he told me that the American Association for Adult Education was having a conference in New York in a month or so, and I should go. I did, and I was impressed with the quality of the people I met there—many of them rebels from the lockstep curricula of academia, including Harry and Bonarro Overstreet, Eduard Lindeman, Will Durant, Frederick Keppel, and Charles Beard. I decided then and there that I felt much more comfortable with and inspired by people like this than I would with diplomats. When the State Department notified me in 1938 that it now had openings, I replied that I had changed my career; I was now an adult educator.

In 1940, after I had been with the NYA for five years, I was waited upon by a "selection committee" from the Boston YMCA inquiring whether I would be interested in becoming director of adult education and organizing an "Association School" for adults. I felt that there were few remaining challenges at the NYA, so I accepted the invitation eagerly. My immediate supervisor was Les Updegraph, the head of the program department, whose managerial style was to delegate, encourage, and support. I did a needs and interests survey of the YMCA members and their families and a sample of people in the surrounding neighborhood and developed an initial program of ten courses that met one evening a week for ten weeks, starting in September 1940. The response was enthusiastic, and we had to divide a couple of the courses into two sections. At Les Updegraph's suggestion, I organized an advisory council consisting of one person elected by the participants in each course. This proved to be both a rich source of ideas about other courses and an aggressive promotion and public relations mechanism. The number of courses just about doubled each ten-week term until all the meeting rooms were solidly booked.

An experience during the spring term of 1941 gave me one of my deepest insights about how to select instructors for adult learners. One day in April three young men appeared in my office and said that they would be interested in a course on astronomy. I assured them that I would try to find an instructor for the fall term. Where does one find an instructor in astronomy? At a university department of astronomy, naturally. So I called Harlow Shapley, director of the Harvard Observatory, and told him about my need. He immediately recommended his teaching assistant ("He needs the money") and put him on the line. He agreed to teach a course starting the following September.

Twelve people registered for the course and showed up at the first session. Several times that evening I looked through the little window in the door of the meeting room to see what was happening. Each time I saw the teaching assistant reading the notes he had developed for an undergraduate course in astronomy at Harvard. And I noticed students' heads starting to nod. At the second session only six students showed up and at the third session only three. I had to close the class, and the registration fees were refunded.

Knowing that there were at least twelve people in Boston who were interested in astronomy, I decided that the problem was with the instructor, not the subject. So I asked myself, "Where might I find a person who knows about astronomy but can teach it in a way that will keep adult learners interested?" When I put this question to Les Updegraph, he responded, "You might try the New England Association of Amateur Astronomers. I looked up the phone number in the yellow pages and called. When I explained the situation to the lady who answered, she said, "Oh, you should talk with Mr. Hadley, the retired chairman of New England's largest utility company and a long-time member of our association," and she gave me his phone number. I called that number and a butler answered. When Mr. Hadley came on the line, he suggested that I come see him at his home.

The taxi pulled up in front of a huge mansion in Brookline. The butler answered the doorbell, and an elderly man with sparkling eyes and flowing white hair ran up to greet me. When I told him what the program was like and about my previous experience with an instructor, he said, "I'd love to try sharing with others what I know about the heavens, but I have had no training or experience as a teacher." I assured him that I would help, and he agreed.

I called the twelve people who had enrolled in the previous course and explained that I had found a new instructor and that a new course would be offered starting in January. All agreed to give it a try, with the registration fee being postponed until the third week. On the evening of the opening meeting the skies were clear but it was bitter cold. Mr. Hadley positioned himself at the door of his meeting room and asked the students as they arrived to keep their coats on since they would be going outdoors. I got my coat, too, as I wanted to see what was going to happen. When all twelve students had assembled, Mr. Hadley said, "Follow me," and took the elevator to the top floor. He led us up a stairway to the roof and said, "Look up at the heavens and tell me what you are curious about." One student said, "Up there toward the north there appear to be several stars that form some sort of shape." I saw Mr. Hadley write on a pad he was carrying, *Constellation* and *Big Dipper*. Another student pointed in another direction and said, "That star seems to be brighter than the others." Mr. Hadley wrote *Venus*.

After some fifteen minutes Mr. Hadley's pad was just about full, and he said, "OK, let's go downstairs; we have our agenda." I sat in on the course for the rest of the evening and was intrigued with how Mr. Hadley engaged the students in exploring what constellations are and their astronomical history, meaning, and significance. The students were obviously deeply involved and had many other observations and questions about constellations. At the end of the period, Mr. Hadley said, "Time's up. Next week we'll move to the next items on the agenda." At the second session eighteen people showed up—the original twelve had passed the word to friends that this was a course that was different.

I learned from this experience—and Mr. Hadley— that enthusiastic amateurs can be superior teachers of adult learners. It also reinforced my growing conviction that you start with adult learners where they are starting from in terms of interests, questions, problems, and concerns.

I had short stints in 1943 as director of the USO in Detroit and between 1934 and 1944 as a communications officer in the U.S. Navy. The chief educational outcome of my naval experience was that my typing speed increased to sixty words a minute, which contributed greatly to my future productivity as a writer. I also had a good deal of time between assignments to read the then existing books on adult education—particularly, Lindeman's *The Meaning of Adult Education*, Lyman Bryson's *Adult Education*, James Truslow Adams's *Frontiers of American Culture*, Ralph Beals and Leon Brody's *The Literature of Adult Education*, Morse Cartwright's *Ten Years of Adult Education*, Mary Ely's *Adult Education in Action*, and Edward Thorndike's *Adult Learning*. It was at this time also that I decided to further my career in adult education through graduate study. I surveyed the twelve graduate programs in adult education in existence at that time and decided on the University of Chicago.

I needed a job to support my wife and son while I was attending the University of Chicago on the G.I. Bill. So I wrote the general secretary of the Chicago YMCA that I was available. Fortunately for me, the YMCA College had decided some time before to move out and become the independent Roosevelt University, leaving three floors of classrooms and offices in the YMCA building bare. When the general secretary got my letter, he called me and asked if I could fill those rooms with informal courses. I said, "Of course." I was mustered out of the navy in May 1946, moved to Chicago, and started work as the director of adult education at Central YMCA on June 1. We gave the adult education program the title "Learning for Living," and within a couple of years it grew until all classrooms were full every evening. It became my second laboratory for experimenting with new ideas and techniques, and experiment I did.

On June 2, 1946, I was accepted into the graduate program of adult education at the University of Chicago and started my first class on June 6. My adviser was Cyril O. Houle, chairman of the Department of Adult Education and dean of University College, which was located in the YMCA building. Houle was without question the leading adult educator in this country at the time. He taught only in seminars (no lecture courses), and I experienced the feeling that I was being treated as an adult and as a valuable resource for the learning of my peers (and for Houle) from the outset. I learned a great deal from the experience of my fellow students, who were drawn from the wide spectrum of adult educational institutions. But Houle's deep commitment to scholarship and his role modeling a rigorous scholarly approach to learning stand out in my mind as probably the most important contribution to my development at the University of Chicago. His attitude toward students is exemplified in the inscription he made in the copies of his books he sent me for years: "To Malcolm Knowles, from whom I have learned so much!"

Another major influence during my University of Chicago days was Carl Rogers. Early in my master's degree program I enrolled in a seminar in group counseling under Professor Arthur Shedlin, an associate of Carl Rogers. I was shocked at what happened in the first meeting. Some fifteen people were sitting around the seminar table when I showed up about five minutes late. They were chatting with neighbors, and after about another ten minutes I noticed some of them looking at their watches. Finally one person said to the whole group, "If the teacher doesn't show up by fifteen minutes after the hour isn't the course supposed to be cancelled?" Another member of the group said, "You are concerned that the teacher is letting us down?" "Yes," said the first speaker. Another person said, "Shouldn't one of us go talk with the dean?" The same member of the group who had responded to the first speaker said, "You feel the dean should know about this deprivation?" "Yes." After a few minutes more of this kind of interaction one of the students pointed to the person who had been responding and shouted, "You're Arthur Shedlin." Shedlin acknowledged that he was, and the rest of the afternoon was spent with the students probing him about his role and his reflecting their feelings and thoughts.

When the seminar adjourned at six o'clock I ran to the library and checked out all the books and periodicals I could find by or about Carl Rogers, I was so curious to find out what this man was all about. I never read so many books and worked so hard in any course I had ever taken. I had never before experienced taking so much responsibility for my own learning as I did in that seminar. It was exhilarating. I began to sense what it means to get "turned on" to learning. I began to think about what it means to be a facilitator of learning rather than a teacher.

Entering the National Scene

I received my M.A. degree in 1949 and my Ph.D. in 1960—working full-time at the YMCA and taking one or two courses each quarter. (Houle helped me meet the residence requirement of three courses per quarter for three quarters by having me take one or two independent study courses in addition to the one or two courses requiring attendance.) Early in this period I joined the American Association for Adult Education and the Department of Adult Education of the National Educational Association and became active in both, attending their conferences and serving on committees. Members of both organizations started bringing pressure on them to amalgamate so as to provide a unified voice for the field. They created a joint commission to study this proposition and make recommendations, and I was appointed to it (I think Houle must have exerted some influence here, too). In 1948 the commission recommended that both organizations be dissolved and a new organization, the Adult Education Association of the U.S.A., be created. This action was taken at a founding assembly in 1951, with the newly founded Fund for Adult Education of the Ford Foundation agreeing to give initial financial support.

The new organization now needed an executive director, preferably one who was not overly identified with either the essentially university constituency of the American Association or the essentially public school constituency of the NEA department. The selection committee was headed by Herbert Hunsaker, the retiring executive director of the American Association, and Leland Bradford, executive director of the NEA department—both of whom I had come to know well as a member of the joint commission. The committee, making a case for a YMCA adult educator's being an ideal "neutral" candidate, nominated me, and I was elected by the executive committee. I started the new position in the fall of 1951.

Another major influence in shaping me as an adult educator at about the same time was the National Training Laboratories and its founding trio, Kenneth Benne, Leland Bradford, and Ronald Lippitt. I had had a course in group dynamics with Herbert Thelen at the University of Chicago in 1949 and became intrigued with the concept of an unstructured group laboratory approach to learning interpersonal attitudes and skills and, particularly, to learning to receive feedback about my behavior nondefensively. So I attended the 1952 summer session of NTL in Bethel, Maine, as the cotrainer of a T-group. I returned as the administrator of the summer session in 1954. My wife and children participated in labs both times, and our family relations were greatly enriched. The insights I gained from these experiences, but particularly from the models of behavior provided by Ken, Lee, and Ron, have been among the most potent components of my professional equipment ever since.

My performance as administrative coordinator (later, executive director) of the Adult Education Association was greatly influenced by the "participative management" theories that were beginning to evolve in those days, largely through the influence of Kurt Lewin and his followers, especially the National Training Laboratories leaders. Policies were supposed to emerge from the grass roots and move up. The role of the leader (me) was essentially twofold: (1) to keep the membership informed about current conditions and possible future developments and (2) to manage the processes that involved the membership in formulating and expressing their desires and wills. As a result, I wrote many articles, annual reports, and letters-to-members to keep members informed and to motivate them to action. Our monthly magazine, *Adult Leadership,* and quarterly journal of research and theory, *Adult Education,* followed this same pattern. A great deal of energy was expended by the board, committees, and staff in helping local, state, and regional associations to become organized. Our national conferences were largely focused on organizational policy issues and were highly participative. There was very little talking down to the troops and a good deal of encouragement to dream. I visualized our mission as being to build a strong membership organization that would be the engine for a vital and growing adult education movement in the United States.

In retrospect, I believe that this foundation laying for a new organization is what was needed at the time, and I resigned as executive director in 1959, satisfied that I had accomplished my mission reasonably well. But most important, in my eight years with the AEA I learned more of what adult education is all about in this country (and in the world) than is taught in all the graduate courses combined.

The Professorial Years

When I knew in 1959 that I would receive my Ph.D. from the University of Chicago in 1960 (at age forty-seven—so have hope, you late bloomers!), I let it be known through my contacts across the country that I was available for an appointment as a professor of adult education. Fortunately, a year earlier Boston University had created a faculty committee "to consider the role and responsibility of the university in adult education." As luck would have it, three of the seven members of the committee were old friends of mine from the AEA and NTL: Kenneth Benne, director of the Human Relations Center, Max Goodson, dean of the School of Education, and Wendell-Yeo, vice-president for academic affairs. The committee submitted a report to the president on March 5, 1959, which called for a "bold new program of adult education." The report recommended ten principles on which the program should be based, the flavor of which is conveyed by these two:

2. A bold program in adult education cannot be completely defined *a priori;* for while precise definition circumscribes properly and meets the niceties of academia and its degree programs, the conditions of dynamic contemporary life are explosive and require an operational blend of the theoretical and the pragmatic.

9. Bold thinking about required educational programs comes from men and women with convictions—convictions based on intelligence and knowledge as well as faith; hence, these are not timid people, and do not assume that their students are or should become timid men and women. If such education truly seeks to inculcate the values of the inquiring mind and the independent, "autonomous" or creative person, it will embrace controversial topics, seek to teach with freedom and inner security, and assert the need for encouraging and informing initiative for social as well as technological innovations and advances.

A few weeks after my "availability" message went out, I received a call from Dean Goodson asking me to come for interviews with the selection committee; within days I was appointed associate professor of adult education with tenure. What a lucky fellow I am. I know of no other professor of adult education who entered into launching a new graduate program with such a resounding mandate.

I began my new role as a full-time professor in the fall of 1960 with some trepidation: would I fit into the world of scholarship after years of performing as a practitioner? I knew I was a good teacher; my experience in teaching courses at George Williams College and elsewhere assured me on that point. But would I be a good professor? My anxiety was no doubt deepened by an episode that took place at the University of Chicago shortly after I had let it be known to the faculty that I had accepted the B.U. position. One of the

faculty members who knew me well took me aside to prepare
me for what he perceived to be a major transition in role.
"Malcolm," he said in effect, "you must realize that you have
to behave differently as a professor. Professors have to be dignified, even somewhat aloof. You can't go around with your
arms around students and hugging them like YMCA secretar-
ies and association executives do. You have to be very proper
and reserved. And, above all, you have to adhere to the rules,
regulations, policies, standards, and procedures of academia
rigorously. You can't be soft-hearted and bend them just
because they may inflict some hardships on some students."

When I arrived at Boston University, I was notified that
the registrar had already received applications for admission
to the new program from some thirty people, and I started
interviewing them at once. I was impressed with the quality
of the applicants' credentials on paper. Almost all of them
had responsible positions—most of them full-time—and some
years of experience as teachers, counselors, and administrators
in a variety of institutions providing some sort of educational
services to adults. I had to repress my enthusiasm and be
dignified with them. I organized a seminar for the fall semester and two courses for the spring semester as a way to get to
know them better and also as a way to get them started before
being admitted to candidacy. I limited enrollment to twenty,
and each course reached its limit. I wrote the course descriptions to sound stuffily academic but actually organized them
around student-planned projects.

During the spring semester several of the applications
for admission to our program came before the Admissions
Committee of the School of Education, complete with Graduate Record Exam or Miller Analogy Test scores, grade
transcripts, and letters of recommendation. Several of the
applications were rejected by the committee because the GRE
scores were below a predetermined minimum. I protested that
other evidence, such as achievement in work experience, professional publications, and letters of recommendation—plus
my own experience with them in my courses—indicated that
they had the ability to do academic work at the graduate

level. But the committee held that "academic standards" must be maintained. I knew for a fact that these people were superior students, and I wanted them in the program. So I wrote an appeal to the graduate committee of the university, making a case for the fact that adults who have been away from academia for several years do not do as well on timed tests as younger students (adults would rather be right than fast, whereas youth would rather be fast than right). I suggested that these students be allowed to take the MAT tests again without a time limit. The committee rejected this suggestion (again in the name of "academic standards") but authorized me to submit petitions to the admissions committee for a waiver of this requirement in individual cases, with strong supportive evidence of other sorts of their ability to perform academically. I did submit petitions of waiver for these applicants, and all but one were accepted.

By the end of this first year I felt so incongruent playing the role of a traditional professor and fighting "academic standards" that were irrelevant to mature, experienced practitioners that I was tempted to resign. But I decided to stay one more year and see what happened when I operated according to principles of adult learning. What I discovered was that the university didn't care what happened in my own classrooms so long as I turned in grades at the end of the semester and didn't intrude on other professors' turf. So I started experimenting with competency-based course syllabi, self-diagnosis of learning needs, student-initiated learning projects, learning contracts, performance assessments rather than tests, and other innovations. The students became excited about being given a share of responsibility for their own learning and provided convincing and creative evidence that they were accomplishing the objectives of the courses. Word spread through the adult educational circles of New England (and beyond) that here was a program that "practiced what it preached," and applications began flooding in. Enrollments increased to the point that we had to add one faculty member (Eugene DuBois) to the program, then another (Frank Pilecki). When I resigned from B.U. in 1974, the program had more than 150 candidates for Ed.D. degrees. I also experienced increasing interest in and support for what we were doing from other faculty members, and a number of them modified their programs to be more congruent with the andragogical model.

My fourteen years at Boston University were years of tremendous growth for me. I learned a good deal about university politics and how "academic standards" often interfere with learning. Perhaps most important, I had a living laboratory in which to test the andragogical model; by the time I left, I had refined it to the point that I felt it was at least a sound basis for further research and theorizing. Substantively, I gained more information about more aspects of the adult education enterprise from the doctoral dissertations of my students than I could have in any other way.

In the early 1960s the administration of North Carolina State University in Raleigh was considering whether to authorize the establishment of a new graduate program in adult education under the joint auspices of the School of Agriculture and Life Sciences and the School of Education. I was invited to spend a few days in the state investigating the feasibility of such a move. After I had conducted interviews with key people in typical institutions providing adult educational services, it became clear that there was a pressing need for a graduate program, and I recommended that one be established as soon as possible. A young faculty member at the University of Wisconsin, Edgar J. Boone, was appointed head of the new department. He was an energetic entrepreneur and quickly built a thriving empire. During the next few years he asked me to conduct occasional faculty-development workshops for his growing cadre of new faculty members, and they started calling me their nonresident guru.

One day in March 1974, Ed called me and asked, "How would you like to come down here and be our resident guru?" When I asked what the job description was, he replied, "Come and do whatever you want to do so long as you continue to help us with staff development." With that kind of freedom in prospect, I said, "I'm on my way" and started in my new position that summer.

I began teaching my favorite courses totally on the andragogical model, advising a growing number of doctoral students and having plenty of time for research, writing, and continuing my workshop and consulting practice across the country. I experienced some resistance to deviations from traditional academic standards from the graduate committee of the university, but Ed Boone arranged for me to be elected to that committee "so I could educate them." I found them to be surprisingly open to learning how this "new clientele" of higher education was different from traditional students. I am sure it helped that by this time I had gained a reputation as being a "respectable" leader of this new field of graduate study, but I felt strong support from my colleagues on the faculty of the School of Education.

My chief areas of growth during this period were in sharpening my abilities as a mentor and facilitator of learning, refining the process of contract learning, and deepening my theoretical foundations. I was the chairman for a number of outstanding doctoral students who greatly broadened my knowledge base through their dissertation research. I retired in 1979 under the university's mandatory retirement policy at age sixty-five.

Life Begins at Retirement

For a number of years I had been building a growing "moonlighting" business—mostly on weekends, vacations, and holidays, although the University of North Carolina system encourages the faculties of its professional schools to spend one weekday each week in practicing their professions in the "real" world. So my "retirement" was more a change of career to full-time consulting and workshopping. The big difference I experienced was that I no longer was tied to any kind of regular schedule, so I was free to get up and go at any time.

The client systems I was invited to work with were richly diverse, including corporations, government agencies, religious institutions, voluntary organizations, and professional associations. Most of my time was spent, however, doing faculty-development workshops with community colleges, colleges and universities, and, occasionally, public schools. In the early years the academic units I worked with were primarily those serving adults: university extension and agricultural extension divisions, evening colleges, and external degree programs. Interestingly, in recent years I have been asked to do workshops on "Understanding and Working with Adult Learners" with traditional undergraduate, graduate, and professional school faculties. I attribute this shift to the rapid growth in the number of adults who are being admitted to regular degree programs as the pool of teenage students shrinks.

During the first few years of serving organizational needs, I began to feel the loss of continuing contact with individual students, and so I joined the faculties of external degree programs—for one year with the Center for Higher Education of Nova University and ever since with the Human and Organizational Development Program of the Fielding Institute, headquartered in Santa Barbara, California, and the Union Graduate School, headquartered in Cincinnati, Ohio. I have been the "adjunct professor" for half a dozen Union Graduate School students and the "mentor" for about thirty Fielding Institute students. I have found them to be the most highly motivated, able, and challenging students I have ever had.

Since shortly after my retirement, every six months I have duplicated and sent copies of my itinerary to relatives, close friends, my stockbroker, and—most important—the students for whom I was a mentor or assessor, so they would know when I could not be reached. I hope that the reproduction of my itinerary for the first quarter of 1984 will give a taste of the flavor of my life in retirement:

Itinerary for Malcolm Knowles, January 1–March 31, 1984

Jan. 5. Miami Valley Presidents' Round Table, Dayton, Ohio: workshop, "Optimizing Human Resources Development."

Jan. 7. Nova University Cluster meeting, Fort Bragg, N.C.

Jan. 11. *National College of Education, Evanston, Ill.: Human Resource Advisory Council meeting.

Jan. 12–14. *Fielding Institute homecoming, Santa Barbara, Calif.: presentation, "The Future of Nontraditional Study.

Feb. 1. Jewish Hospital, Cincinnati, Ohio: workshop on adult learning for in-service education staff.

Feb. 4. Nova University Cluster meeting, Fort Bragg, N.C.

Feb. 7–8. Fielding Institute, Lincoln, Neb.: public workshop, "Understanding and Working with Adult Learners."

Feb. 11–12. Kearney State College, Kearney, Neb.: faculty-development workshop.

Feb. 18–19. Fielding Institute, Raleigh, N.C.: human development seminar.

Mar. 10. Fielding Institute fair, Chapel Hill, N.C.

Mar. 16–17. Oklahoma State University, Oklahoma City: weekend graduate course.

Mar. 19–23. *Fielding Institute, Santa Barbara, Calif.: admissions and contract workshop.

Mar. 27. *Fielding Institute, San Diego, Calif.: public workshop on adult learning.

Mar. 30. Methodist Hospitals of Memphis: in-service education workshop.

Mar. 31. St. Mary College, Leavenworth, Kan.: faculty workshop.

Clearly, I have been busier since I retired than I ever was while holding a full-time job, but it has been a period of expansive growth. I have met hundreds of able, smart, and nice people all over the country and the world, and I have

---

*Asterisks indicate trips on which Hulda was with me; in May 1986, she suffered a stroke, which made it impossible for her to travel with me thereafter.

learned more from them than they have from me. It is from them that I have learned how organizations really work and how dependent they are on effective programs of human resources development. These people have kept me in touch with innovative developments that are occurring daily in the real world of adult educational practice.

But these have also been years of voluminous reading and writing. I haven't minded the traveling because I get so much reading done on airplanes and in airports and motel rooms. I have read one major book a week, on average, whereas when I was a full-time professor, I was lucky to finish one a month. My mind has been exposed to—and has incorporated or adapted—systems theory, transpersonal psychology, computerized information processing, advances in knowledge about how the brain functions, futurism, and many other frontiers of the knowledge explosion and technological revolution we are exploring.

I have also had time to write, producing two books and about sixty articles, book reviews, and book chapters in the first nine years of retirement.

I can't imagine a better, richer life.

Chapter 2

Eight Episodes
That Changed My Life

I suppose many people have had an experience or a flash of insight that brought together things that previously had seemed disconnected or that changed the direction of their lives. I have identified eight such "insight episodes" that I have not cited in other chapters in this book but would like to share with you.

Learning to Be a Writer

Actually, I started writing rather early in life—writing for publication, that is. My first article was published when I was sixteen: "How to Earn Fifty Merit Badges," *Boys' Life,* October 29, 1929. A little over a year earlier this magazine of the Boy Scouts of America had announced that a free trip to the world jamboree in Berkinhead, England, would be awarded to the scout who had earned the most merit badges in the following nine months. I decided I wanted this prize and could figure out a fail-safe way to get it. My solution was to get a large piece of wallboard and draw horizontal and vertical lines on it so that it contained 270 squares—one square for each day for nine months. Then in each box I entered what I would have to do that day to earn credit toward a given merit badge. (Today this would be called a modified PERT chart.) I installed this chart on a wall opposite my bed, and every morning when I woke up I would check what was scheduled for that day. A few weeks before the nine months were up, I had been awarded fifty merit badges and won the trip to England. I thought the technique might be useful to other Boy Scouts, so I wrote the article and it was accepted by *Boys' Life.*

In the spring of 1929, in preparation for my trip to England, I convinced the editor of our daily paper, the *Palm Beach Post,* that it would help his circulation if I wrote a daily column describing the experiences our troop was having at the world jamboree. I was paid a few cents a column inch, so you can be certain that my reports were rich in detail.

During my senior year I was editor of the Palm Beach High School News and wrote an editorial entitled "A Memorial That Means Something," praising the senior class for voting to "turn its efforts and energies to aiding in financing the ninth month of school, which under present county school board financial conditions will be impossible except for aid from sources other than tax collections," instead of producing a class annual. That editorial won second prize for editorials from the National Honorary Society for High School Journalists and was reproduced in *Best Creative Work in American High Schools, 1929–1930.*

While I was director of training for the National Youth Administration for Massachusetts I wrote an article, "This Job-Hunting System Works," that was published in *Your Life* (a forerunner of *Psychology Today*) in August 1939. And, of course, during my tenure with the NYA I wrote a number of internally published reports and brochures.

Toward the end of my work as director of adult education at the Boston YMCA I wrote an article, "Having Any Fun?" in which I extolled the virtues of evening classes (such as those at the YMCA) as a source of life-expanding pleasure. This article was published in *Holiday* in September 1946.

During those seventeen years I had published four articles in popular periodicals. I was beginning to think of myself as a writer but realized that I was by no means a master of the craft. I think my articles were accepted because I had something useful to say, not because of the grace of their prose. I had gained some helpful tips from seeing what editors had done to my manuscripts, but I had no sense of style. In 1946 I enrolled in the graduate program in adult education at the University of Chicago and became exposed to the writing of Cyril O. Houle, one of the most graceful writers I had encountered. I asked him about his secret, and he referred me to Rudolph Flesch's (1949) *The Art of Readable Writing.* The big learning I got from this classic was to write as one talks—converse with people rather than write for an abstract audience—and to use simple sentences with active verbs. This made good sense to me, but I couldn't quite figure out how to do it.

Then something happened one day in 1948 that was the turning point in my career as a writer. I was working on my master's thesis, which was an analysis of contemporary practices in program planning and teaching in adult education. One day Cyril Houle was having lunch with the editor of Association Press, the publication arm of the national YMCA—at that time a principal publisher of adult educational materials. The editor asked Cy if he or any of his students had any works in progress that he thought Association Press might be interested in looking at. Cy mentioned my thesis and said he thought I had an outline and a couple of chapters done. The editor asked to see them, and I rushed them over to Cy's office. After looking at them, the editor said that, yes, he would like to see the manuscript when it was completed.

During the next several days I tried to write the next chapter of what was now both a master's thesis and a potential book. I would write a few paragraphs, read them, and then rip them out of the typewriter and throw them into the wastebasket. The evening of the third or fourth day of this behavior I went down to our living room and plopped myself in a chair, obviously dejected. Hulda asked me what was wrong, and I explained that I was blocking in writing the master's thesis/book. She said, "I know that you are writing the master's thesis for Cy Houle, but for whom are you writing the book? Name three people you think are in the target audience for a book." I named Louise Hamil, a very conscientious and practical director of adult education in the Mobile, Alabama, public schools; Adolph Adolphson, the sophisticated dean of university extension at the University of Wisconsin; and Mary Settle, director of volunteer training for the American Red Cross.

This gave me the idea of writing to those three people and Cy and asking them to send me a head photo. When all four pictures has arrived about a week later, I took them up to my study and taped them to the wall in front of my typewriter. After typing a few paragraphs I would look at Louise's picture and say, "Is this clear and down to earth enough for you?" If she nodded yes, I would look at Adolph and say, "Is this sophisticated and operational enough for you?" If he nodded yes, I would turn to Mary and say, "Is this relevant to volunteer training?" If she responded that it was, I would turn to Cy and ask, "Is this scholarly enough for you?" If he responded affirmatively, I would go on to the next page or two. All of a sudden my fingers started racing; they could hardly keep up with the conversation that was going on. I finished my master's thesis/book in record time.

My master's degree was awarded in 1949, and the book, my first, was published in 1950 under the title *Informal Adult Education*. In the thirty-seven years since then I have written 16 books and 191 articles. Or, more accurately, I have talked them.

I have told this story to a number of former students and colleagues, and many of them have told me that when they started to write by talking to real people, the floodgates of communication opened for them, too. I no longer have to have photographs in front of me, but before I start writing a book or an article I picture in my mind a representative sample of the people I want to talk with. I no longer write a book; I talk a book. Have I been communicating with you, Tom, Betsy, Paul, and Becky?

Marrying Hulda

During my junior year at Harvard I was the general secretary of the Model League of Nations of New England.

One of my fellow officers was a Wellesley junior named Betty. One day she asked me if I would like to be her date at a formal dance at Wellesley, and I accepted with enthusiasm. A couple of weeks before the date of the dance she called me to say that she had forgotten that she had invited a student from M.I.T. to the dance several months before, so she couldn't take me. But, she said, she could get me a date with a sopho- more who lived in her house if I wanted. The classmate's name was Hulda Fornell, who, she raved, was a beautiful and brilliant girl who had been born in Sweden. I had a romantic notion about Swedish girls, and I accepted her offer.

When Betty introduced me to Hulda at the dance, I was moonstruck. Hulda was, indeed, a beautiful blonde blue-eyed Swedish-looking girl with a cute turned-up nose. She was short (5'1") but, as we used to say in those days, well stacked. And I was in my short-girl phase. When we started dancing, the starched shirt of my tuxedo kept popping out and hitting her bosom. She would laugh and say that was cute, and it made the general secretary of the New England Model League of Nations seem less stuffy. When she laughed, her eyebrows rose and made pretty little creases in her forehead. As we talked, I learned that her father was a tool-and-die maker in the automotive industry in Detroit and that he and his family had immigrated to America in 1922, when Hulda was nine. In Sweden he had been active in the cooperative movement and was now active in the labor union movement in Detroit. As we talked about the social issues of the day—the Great Depression, high unemployment, the New Deal, and the like—it became clear that our value systems were identical. When I learned that she had been the spelling champion of Michigan when she was thirteen, just four years after coming to this country, my mind was made up. I needed a good speller in my life.

Hulda and I started "going steady" and grew more and more fond of each other. Two years after we met, she gradu- ated and we were married, on August 20, 1935. I was working at the National Youth Administration of Massachusetts and earning $22 a week. She got a job at the Boston YWCA pay-

ing $15 a week. That hardly seems like living wages these
days, but at that time tenderloin steak was selling for something like 29 cents a pound, and we actually started a savings
account.

While I was developing program materials and promotional brochures at the NYA, Hulda was my copyreader and
greatly improved the editorial quality of the publications—
including correcting a number of spelling errors. When I was
considering making a move to become the director of adult
education at the Boston YMCA, she encouraged me to "take
a risk, seek an adventure, have a growth experience." In 1941
our son, Eric, was born and Hulda became a full-time home-
maker and mother. I learned a lot from her in the next few
years about the art of nurturing; she was a supportive and
yet challenging mother. In 1944, when I was thinking about
enlisting in the navy, she again encouraged me to stretch into
new challenges, and she and Eric followed me to my various
posts in Plattsburg, New York, and Oceanside and San Diego,
California. While I was recuperating from an ulcer episode
in the Camp Pendleton hospital in Oceanside in 1945, Hulda
arranged for the Oceanside public library to get several books
on adult education for me, including Alvin Johnson's *The
Cloak of History*. It became clear to me that she was my chief
source of intellectual, not to mention moral and psychic,
support.

When I was retired from the navy in 1946, there was no
question about our moving to Chicago so that I could take
up the post of director of adult education at the YMCA and
enroll in the graduate program of adult education at the
University of Chicago—in spite of the negative impressions
we had of Chicago as a place to live. Actually, we were very
happy living in Evanston and Wilmette. (When I expressed
some reservations about returning to the YMCA, Hulda said,
"I like the YMCA; the people there may be smart or dumb,
fat or skinny, tall or short, but you can count on their being
people of goodwill.") Our daughter, Barbara, was born in
Evanston shortly after we moved there in 1946. As I developed
program materials and promotional brochures for the Chi-

cago YMCA adult education program, Hulda again served as my trusted copyeditor and proofreader, as she was when I started working on my master's thesis and book, *Informal Adult Education,* in 1948.

Hulda, Eric, Barbara, and I attended the National Laboratories summer session in Bethel, Maine, in 1952 and 1954, and became hooked on human relations training, group dynamics, and leadership training. I began doing workshops for adult educational organizations, business and industry, government agencies, and voluntary organizations; Hulda did workshops with the League of Women Voters, church groups, the YWCA, and others. Some workshops we did together, with Hulda taking special responsibility for observing what was happening to individuals and I taking special responsibility for observing group behavior. We found that this division of labor paid extra dividends in terms of training effectiveness.

In 1954 the editor of Association Press asked me if I would do a small book on leadership development aimed primarily at a voluntary organization audience. I agreed provided that Hulda and I could be joint authors, and he thought that was a great idea. In the early stages of our planning and writing the book we had occasional disagreements about what we should say or how we should say it. Hulda insisted on absolute honesty—no embellishments on what was known or what happened. I had a tendency to want to make a good set of facts or a good example better by dressing it up. She usually convinced me that honesty was the best policy. The little book, *How to Develop Better Leaders,* was published in 1955 and received enthusiastic reviews.

The next year the Association Press editor told us that he was picking up signals that the literature on group dynamics, which was proliferating at that time, was too difficult and academic for many readers. He asked us if we would be willing to write another small book, an easy-to-understand guide to that literature and its main findings (what in high school Latin class we called a pony). We collaborated again, this time more harmoniously, and produced *Introduction to*

Group Dynamics, published in 1959. It got rave reviews, one reviewer calling it "the little gem," and for about ten years it sold more copies each year than the previous year—an unusual happening in the publishing industry. It was revised and updated for Cambridge Book Company in 1972 and is still selling.

A couple of years after I moved to Boston University in 1960 and our daughter entered junior high, Hulda decided to enter the master's degree program in guidance and counseling at Boston University. Upon graduation she was appointed a guidance counselor at Newton South High School, within a couple of miles of where we were living. She quickly became recognized as a superior counselor and received numerous accolades (honestly you did, honey; I'm not embellishing). She also became my in-house consultant and resource person on understanding individual behavior. When I moved to North Carolina State University in Raleigh in 1974, she decided to retire and so was able to go with me on many of my trips. We have been to England, Denmark, Sweden, France, Germany, Guatemala, Venezuela, Brazil, Japan, New Zealand, Australia, South Korea, Hong Kong, Singapore, and Bangkok together—not to mention to Canada many times. Hulda has been a constant source of both psychic support and substantive assistance during most of my life.

Learning to Be Authentic

During my graduate studies at the University of Chicago, when I was strongly under the influence of Carl Rogers and his associate Arthur Shedlin, I was exposed to the concept of behaving authentically. In fact, I found Rogers's three characteristics of the effective helper to be fundamental: (1) unqualified positive regard for the helpee, (2) a deep ability to empathize—to think and feel *with* rather than *about* a helpee, and (3) absolute authenticity—to behave out of your real personhood rather than out of some role. I began reflecting that while I was the director of training of the National Youth Administration of Massachusetts I frequently behaved as an agent of the government and justified my actions as being required by governmental policies and standards. As the director of adult education of the YMCAs of Boston, Detroit, and Chicago I frequently behaved as the agent of a Christian Association and took stands that I really didn't believe in.

I also recalled that when I was the executive director of the Adult Education Association of the U.S.A., I was terribly impressed with Ronald Lippitt's self-assurance and brilliance, with Kenneth Benne's philosophical approach to things, and with Alvin Zander's absolute artistry with large meetings. I tried to be like them and several times fell flat on my face because people didn't respond to me the way they did to them. Toward the end of my tenure with the AEA it began to dawn on me that I had some unique strengths that were different from theirs. My special strength was that I was an experienced practitioner; they were scholars. I found myself feeling so much more secure—and authentic—when I presented myself and acted as a practitioner.

When, in 1959, I learned that I had been appointed associate professor of education at Boston University starting in 1960, I announced this good news to one of my professors at the University of Chicago. As recounted in Chapter One, he told me I couldn't go around being warm and friendly and putting my arm around people; I had to become dignified, formal, reserved, and authoritative. Over coffee he elaborated on how to play the role of professor.

During my first year at Boston University I tried playing this role, and I was miserable. I felt phony. My self-concept was that of a warm, tender, loving, student-centered person rather than a stuffy professor. At the end of the year I toyed with the idea of resigning and going back into voluntary association administration, where I could be natural. But I decided to stay a second year and see what I could get away with by being myself. I started establishing warm relations with students, being supportive rather than judgmental, facilitating their active participation in planning and conducting learning experiences, and even involving them in evaluating themselves. I found that I could get away with almost anything I wanted to do so long as I limited it to my own classroom. I decided I could be a good professor while being myself—with very few compromises—and decided to stay on.

But I was having trouble performing my role of doctoral adviser that way. My eyes were opened to this fact during the beginning of my second year at the university. One day my first doctoral student to reach the dissertation proposal stage came in with the first draft of a proposal and said, "I'd like to know what you think of this." I read it and responded, "I don't think it will get by the committee." He replied, "I don't care about the committee yet—I want to know what you think of it." That rocked me back on my heels, as I realized that I was not responding as my authentic self but was playing the role of the chairman of a committee. I read it again and reacted with observations and suggestions, frequently preceded by the phrase "As I see it." His eyes lit up and he said, "Thanks for the help." Subsequently, I found myself falling into the same trap with two or three other students, and I decided to do something about it. During the next few interviews with doctoral students I asked a second student to sit in and observe me and give me a signal when he or she detected that I was not being authentic (explaining to the student with the proposal that the second student was observing me, not him or her). After three such feedback sessions I had overcome that habit.

This personality transformation was reinforced a few weeks later when I was facilitating a course on group and interpersonal relations, the purpose of which was to help students develop human relations training skills. After an interesting interaction, I said, "Let's stop the action for a moment and analyze what has just happened. I think you can learn something from it." One of the students quickly interjected, "Malcolm, what do you want to learn from it?" I was thrown for a loop again, realizing that I was playing the role of "trainer" rather than being a fellow learner, which was what I had announced my role would be at the beginning of the course. So I said, "I would like to see if I can get some clues as to what kinds of statements produce defensive behavior," and off we went pooling our observations about this phenomenon.

I believe that I have not fallen off the authenticity wagon many times since. I have observed other teachers and trainers and picked up many ideas, techniques, and behaviors from them. But I have tried to adapt them to my personal style rather than to copy them. I make a point in the opening session of a workshop or course to present myself as a human being rather than an authority figure. I describe the positions I have held, but in terms of the experiences they have provided that might serve as resources for learning. At the same time, I emphasize that all the other participants in the workshop or course have also had experiences that can serve as resources for learning—and devote the next block of time to finding out what those experiences are. I further urge the participants to call me Malcolm rather than Dr. Knowles or Professor Knowles, explaining that this will help me be an authentic person and help them to relate to me as a human being.

Overcoming Resistance to Learning

As I have just indicated, one of the courses in our graduate program in adult education at Boston University was a four-semester sequence entitled "Group and Interpersonal Relations." The first semester was a basic human relations training laboratory. In the second semester those students who wanted to continue the sequence (which was most of them) were assigned to be process observers in that semester's basic labs. In the third semester the previous semester's observers became cotrainers in basic labs, and in the fourth semester they served as trainers. During the first year this sequence was offered, several students from the School of Nursing usually enrolled voluntarily. The results were so satisfactory that in the second year the School of Nursing made the sequence mandatory for all nursing students majoring in administration.

Early in the second year it became clear that several of the nursing students were resisting; they didn't participate, and they missed meetings. So I brought all the students together in a general session and said, "I want to be sure that each of you understands the purpose and application to your life of this sequence: (1) to deepen your understanding of your natural behavior in interpersonal relations and its consequences, (2) to sharpen your skills in participating effectively in interpersonal relations, (3) to develop skills in designing and conducting interpersonal relations training activities, and (4) to be able to apply principles of effective interpersonal relations in leadership roles. Now, I understand that some of you are required to be here. I feel bad about that. I wish you were all here because you voluntarily chose to be. But there is nothing you or I can do about that right now—although we might be able to have the requirement removed in the future. I hope that we all can have an enjoyable and productive time together anyway."

It became clear that the resistance was lessening, and eventually it seemed to disappear. My hypothesis is that by making public the fact that I knew some students were there under compulsion, and wished this weren't so, took some of the wind out of the resisters' sails and made it legitimate for them to start getting involved. I have used the same strategy, usually with the same result, in a number of situations since then when I detected that some people were being "sent" to my workshops.

Since that time I have observed or experimented with other ways of overcoming resistance and increasing motivation to learn. One strategy is the use of role models. One of the most dramatic examples of this strategy was in prison education. Some years ago one of my former B.U. students, who had become director of education at a New Jersey correctional institution, invited me to observe an experiment he was trying. He explained that the New Jersey correctional system had adopted a policy of emphasizing the preparation of inmates to function productively after they were released. Those in charge of the facility had instituted a counseling service, but their main hope was in a program of vocational training.

My former student explained that attendance at the vocational courses was good (it was required) but that motivation was poor. The convicts didn't apply themselves, and they didn't learn much. He had identified a former convict who had "made it" outside and had invited him to meet with a group of current inmates and describe his experience to them. I sat to the side of the group with my former student to observe the experiment. The invited guest was dressed in a double-breasted suit with white shirt and tie and exuded success. He began by explaining that the first time he took a drafting and sheet metal course he was not really interested, did not apply himself, just doodled, and didn't learn anything. But as his release date approached, he began to worry about how he would get a job when he was released and decided to take the course again. This time he really applied himself and became a pretty good sheet metal worker. After his release he began making sheet metal objects in his garage and sold them to contractors. The word got around that his products were superior, and he started getting a flood of orders. He had to rent part of a warehouse, buy more equipment, and hire helpers. His business kept growing until he had to rent a whole building and hire dozens more workers. We were meeting in a room with a large window (with bars, of course) that looked out on the parking lot. When he had finished describing his experience, he pointed out the window and said, "See that white Mercedes out there? That's mine."

My former student reported to me some months later that after that experience inmates became really industrious students in their vocational courses and the placement rate in jobs after their release increased substantially.

I developed a somewhat more elaborate variation on the use of role models in the mid-sixties. Hospitals across the country were introducing intensive coronary care units and were running into problems training nurses fast enough to perform in them. The National Institutes of Health gave a substantial grant to the ROCOM division of Hoffman

LaRoche Company to develop a multimedia package that could be used to train general-duty nurses to perform in ICCUs. It was a first-class production that proved effective in pilot tests. The American Heart Association bought a number of copies and donated them to scores of hospitals. Follow-up studies showed that when the hospitals notified their general-duty nurses that the package was available for individual or small-group use, the package usually sat on a shelf.

At this point ROCOM asked me to visit a couple of hospitals and see if I could find out what was wrong and what could be done about it. It didn't take more than half a dozen interviews with general-duty nurses before it became clear that they felt no need for further training. After all, they were already taking care of heart patients on general-duty floors. Obviously, the nurses didn't appreciate the difference between a general-duty floor and the pressure-cooker environment of an ICCU, where an ICCU nurse had to keep half a dozen or more patients under almost constant observation through vertical windows, with oscillographs glowing, red lights flashing, and bells ringing frequently.

My recommendation to ROCOM was that we take a portable movie camera to an ICCU and record what really goes on there. ROCOM agreed, and we filmed perhaps two dozen nurses at work in an ICCU. We chose about a dozen episodes that depicted poor, mediocre, and excellent performances. I arranged for a hospital to let me show the film at a regular nursing staff meeting. I first showed the film straight through, so that they would get an overview of it. Then I told them I would show it again, but this time they were to rate the nurses' (who had been given fictitious names) performances as poor, mediocre, or excellent. When the viewers reported their ratings, it was clear that they had had no trouble rating the ICCU nurses and that there was consensus. I showed the film a third time, and asked the viewers to list the attributes (knowledge, skill, attitude) that the excellent performers seemed to have that the poor and mediocre didn't have. Again, the nurses had no trouble doing this, and we ended up with a list of more than a dozen items, which I

wrote on a chalkboard. Finally, I had the nurses rate themselves individually in terms of the degree to which they pos-
sessed each characteristic on a scale of from 1 (low) to 5
(high). We didn't have them report these ratings, but I saw a
lot of *1*s, *2*s, and *3*s on their sheets.

We then announced that the ROCOM multimedia training package, which dealt with these items, would be available
for individual and small-group viewing twenty-four hours a
day in the in-service education library. That hospital reported
to me after a few weeks that the ICCU training package was
checked out several times a day. We then developed a facilitator's manual for the diagnostic program so that local in-
service education directors could take their staffs through the
process.

I have found several rich sources of information about
other strategies for helping people to become aware of their
learning needs and therefore reduce their resistance and
increase their motivation. Paolo Freire's *Pedagogy of the
Oppressed* (1970) describes techniques that are especially effective with the undereducated. William Pfeiffer and John Jones
have edited a nine-volume series entitled *Handbook of Structured Experiences for Human Relations Training* (1969–) that
presents simulation exercises and other tools for alerting
people to their learning needs. The most comprehensive book
to date on motivational strategies is Raymond Wlodkowski's
Enhancing Adult Motivation to Learn (1985).

Learning About Cross-Cultural Education

During the 1950s, 1960s, and early 1970s, I conducted
several workshops in Puerto Rico, England, France, Guatemala, and Venezuela without ever thinking of them as cross-
cultural educational activities. I simply thought of the participants as being people who were interested in examining the
principles of adult learning and their application to a variety
of adult educational situations. I used the same process design
I used in my workshops in the United States, which is reproduced in Exhibit 1. It clearly involved the participants in

Exhibit 1. Understanding and Working with Adult Learners.

Process Design for a One-Day Workshop

Competency-Development Objectives

1. An understanding of the modern concepts of adult learning and how these differ from traditional concepts of youth learning.

2. An understanding of the role of educator as facilitator and resource for self-directed learners.

3. The ability to apply these concepts to the designing of learning experiences for oneself and others through the use of learning contracts.

Schedule

9:00–10:00 A.M.   Climate-setting exercise
—Sharing of information in small groups about participants' whats, whos, and questions, problems, or issues

10:00–10:15 A.M.   Analysis of this experience and identification of the characteristics of a climate that is conducive to learning

10:15–10:30 A.M.   Break

10:30–11:30 A.M.   Dialogic presentation of the theoretical framework of andragogy

11:30–12:00   Introduction to competency-based education and a model of competencies for facilitators of learning

12:00–1:00 P.M.   Lunch

1:00–1:30 P.M.   Diagnosis of competency-development needs by participants

1:30–2:30 P.M.   Drafting of learning contracts
—Introduction to contract learning
—Individuals' draft contracts for their two or three highest-priority learning objectives
—Individuals review contracts in triads

2:30–2:45 P.M.   Break

2:45–3:30 P.M.   Problem clinic
—Malcolm responds to questions about this process and any unresolved problems and issues

3:30–4:00 P.M.   Evaluation of this workshop

4:00 P.M.   Adjourn

---

sharing responsibility with me—a facilitator of learning—in taking a high degree of responsibility for diagnosing learning needs, formulating learning objectives, and planning, carrying out, and evaluating learning experiences. I found that the participants in these several cultures responded in much the same way the American participants did.

In 1973 I was asked to make a presentation on "Principles of Adult Learning as Applied to Human Resources Development" at the first South American Conference on Human Resources Development in São Paulo, Brazil. My presentation was scheduled for the first day, from 5:00 to 6:00 P.M. The conference started at 9:00 A.M. in a large auditorium with about two thousand people sitting in fixed seats in tiers. Presentations were scheduled one per hour, with a two-hour lunch break. Each presentation was a prepared lecture from a raised platform with a lectern; most of the presenters read from a paper, a few with some overhead transparency slides. Almost all of them ran over their time limit by ten to thirty minutes.

When I was introduced at six o'clock—an hour late—I could see that the audience was glassy-eyed from seven hours of being talked down to. I took the microphone from the podium and walked down from the platform to the level of the auditorium floor, explaining that I felt more comfortable and less stilted when I could see the eyes of the people I was talking with. Then I explained that I wanted to start by applying two cardinal principles of adult education, as I saw them: (1) You always start with learners where they are starting from, in terms of their interests, problems, and concerns; and (2) you engage the learners in a process of active inquiry with you. Then I asked the members of the audience to stand and face three or four of their neighbors and pool their questions about adult learners, with one member of each group volunteering to keep track of the questions and report them out when we got back together. The expressions on their faces showed the relief they felt from even this small change of position and activity.

After about ten minutes of spirited buzzing in their

small groups, I called the audience back together and explained that I would deal with as many questions as I could in the remaining time. I then invited the reporters to raise their hands, and I called on them randomly. The questions were right on target: "How are adults different from youth as learners?" "How do you motivate adults to want to learn?" "How do you find out what adults' learning needs are?" "What are the most effective methods and techniques in working with adult learners?" In response to each question I shared my thoughts and experiences for four or five minutes and then invited members of the audience to add theirs if they wanted to. I was pleased that perhaps a dozen people accepted this invitation during the hour. (I should explain that arrangements had been made for simultaneous translation, so each participant had a headset, and microphones were placed in the aisles.) Promptly at seven o'clock I adjourned the meeting, thanking the participants for their help.

The evaluation forms that were collected at the end of the conference rated this session as the highlight of the program.

That evening four enthusiastic people representing two universities in Brazil asked me whether I would be interested in doing a five-day workshop to introduce the andragogical model to the faculties of their universities the following fall. I said I would be very interested, and we set dates. I told them that I would send them a design for a five-day workshop on "Understanding and Working with Adult Learners" for their reaction. (The design was an extension of the one in Exhibit 1, simply with more time being given to the various activities, plus some practice exercises on performing the role of learning facilitator.)

The first workshop was at the University of Bahia in Salvador, northern Brazil. I had agreed to meet with the program committee on the Friday evening before the Monday opening of the workshop. When I walked into the seminar room in which the meeting was being held, about a dozen people were sitting around a table with Maria, the chairperson, at the head. It was clear to me from the expressions on their faces that something was wrong, and I asked Maria if there was a problem. "Well," she replied, "we have been looking over the process design you sent us and we're afraid that you don't understand Brazilians. You must realize that we are from a Mediterranean culture, in which the teacher is put on a pedestal and the students are trained to listen carefully to the lecture and be deferential. We are afraid that if we stay with this process design, in which the learners are given so much responsibility and you don't lecture, they won't return the second day."

I said to myself, "I can't believe that people aren't people everywhere," but said out loud, "How about our going with the process design the first day and at the end of the day I'll take a vote on how many of the participants want to stay with the process design and how many want to shift to four days of lectures." (In my previous experience with Mediterranean cultures I had found the people to be very expressive, and the process design called for them to spend most of the first day expressing themselves in terms of their background and interests, so I was optimistic about the outcome of the vote.) Maria then added that the committee had opened registration in the workshop to people from government, business and industry, and community organizations; that they had 105 advance registrations; and that she was worried that the process design wouldn't work with so many people. I assured her that I had used this design many times with this many people and that it worked fine so long as we were meeting in a room with good acoustics or floor microphones so the participants could hear one another. The committee agreed to this compromise.

The first day went swimmingly, as I had predicted. My biggest problem was getting the participants to come back to order after I had put them into small groups. I was beginning to get hoarse from shouting, "Let's get back together." So Maria, who had been a physical education teacher, went to her office and got her referee's whistle and the participants quickly quieted down. At the end of the day I explained to them the agreement I had with the committee to poll them on their preference regarding the design. I first asked how many of them wanted to shift to a lecture design, and one hand went up. When I asked how many wanted to stay with the process design, 104 hands went up. So I turned to the one who wanted lectures and said, "OK, Pedro, tomorrow you can come up here and sit with me, and I'll give you lectures while they are working in their groups." He did, and I started a lecture on theories of learning. As I talked, I noticed that he kept turning his head and looking at what was going on at the tables. At the coffee break he said, "Dr. Knowles, would you be insulted if I joined one of those groups?" I said I thought that would be just fine, and he did.

The workshop went smoothly for the remaining four days, with the participants entering into the various activities seriously and with enthusiasm. In the last hour of the fourth day I asked them to get back into their groups of four or five and pool their evaluations of the workshop in terms of its design and their learning outcomes. The general tone of the evaluations was that they experienced being treated as adult learners and learned the attitudes and techniques that would enable them to produce the same results with their clients. One of the table groups was composed of staff members from the national department of education in Brasilia, and their evaluation was different. Their spokesman reported that they agreed that "Malcolm Knowles is more subversive than Paolo Freire, since Freire had the political goal of overthrowing the government as integral to his approach, and therefore the government had a basis for exiling him. Knowles, on the other hand, has no political goals in his andragogical approach, but only the goal of producing self-directed learners. But if we succeed in producing truly self-directed learners, they will know what to do about the government, and it will have no basis for exiling anybody as they did with Freire."

That evening I met again with the program committee to discuss the participants' evaluation and to get theirs. As the meeting opened, Maria said, "Malcolm, I have an apology and an admission to make before we get started. First, I apologize for questioning your understanding of the Brazilian culture when you presented your process design. But more importantly, my admission: I have gained a great insight from this experience, and that is that we Brazilians stereotype ourselves and so close our minds to the fact that we are normal human beings, too." As I was flying from Salvador to Porto Allegre the next day for my second five-day workshop in southern Brazil, I began thinking about the many ways that we Americans also stereotype ourselves. Incidentally, the word had reached Porto Allegre from Salvador that the process design was a great success, so everything went smoothly there.

Now let me make it clear that I don't discount the fact that there are cultural differences that need to be taken into account in interacting with people from different cultures. But my current perception is that these differences are more in terms of customs than in fundamental processes, such as learning. I honor their customs and am willing to adapt to them, but I accept and respect their basic humanity.

Reaching an Understanding of Learning Theories

One day in March 1971, I was sitting peacefully in my office at Boston University when the phone rang. It was Leonard Nadler, an old friend and colleague who was at George Washington University. I knew that he was editing a series of books under the theme "Building Blocks of Human Potential" for Gulf Publishing Company. The reason he was calling, he said, was that he had just realized they had not included a book on learning theory and human resources development in their plans for the series, and he thought that one was needed; would I be interested in writing it? I asked him to hold a minute while I looked at my date book to see what free time I had the next summer. I discovered that I had twenty-one uncommitted days in July and August of 1972 for the final writing, and told him, yes, I would be able to do it and get the manuscript to him on August 23, 1972. He said, "It's a deal."

I decided I had better start reviewing the literature on learning theory, so I went to my bookcase and pulled down my copy of Hilgard and Bower's (1948) *Theories of Learning*, which I had read for one of my courses at the University of Chicago many years earlier. After I had blown the dust off the top, I began reading it and started to have the feelings I recalled having experienced when I first read it. One feeling was that learning theorists—not just Hilgard and Bower, but the theorists they quoted—are terribly dull and abstruse writers. My second feeling was that they are an egotistical lot— each presents his or her theory as the "right" one. A third feeling was that they are a mean bunch of people—they say nasty things about one another. A fourth feeling I had was that Hilgard and Bower didn't know about the learning theorists I had found made most sense—the humanistic theorists such as Rogers and Maslow. They presented only the behaviorist and cognitive theorists.

After I finished scanning the book again, I had the final feeling—that learning theory is a jungle. The impression I had is that there are a score or more fairly discrete and disconnected theories. How in the world could I make sense out of them for human resources development practitioners? I decided I couldn't and tried calling Leonard Nadler to beg off the assignment. However, he was on a trip to the Orient or some other place, so I couldn't reach him.

A few days after making this decision I was sitting in the waiting room of the political science department waiting for a doctoral committee to convene when I noticed a copy of Goulet and Baltes's (1970) *Life-Span Developmental Psychology* open to a chapter entitled "Models of Development and Theories of Development" by Hayne W. Reese and Willis F. Overton. I began reading it, and lights started turning on in my head. A central thesis in the chapter is that all theories are based on some model of the phenomena that the theories are trying to explain. This insight started me asking, what is the model of man that the behaviorists are coming from? And the answer seemed clear: man as machine. It is a reactive, passive, robot or empty-vessel model of man. The purpose of education, therefore, is to program people through stimulus-response mechanisms to behave in predetermined ways.

When I asked myself what is the model of man that the cognitive theorists are coming from, the answer that came to me was man as brain. The distinguishing characteristic of the human species is that they have highly developed brains that are capable of thinking, feeling, learning, and problem solving. The purpose of education is therefore to train the brain to perform those functions efficiently and effectively.

When I asked myself what is the model of man that the humanistic theorists are coming from, the answer was man as living organism. They see human beings as continuously developing, self-directing, holistic organisms with an almost infinite capacity to achieve their unique potential. The purpose of education is to facilitate their development toward that unique potential.

It became clear to me at this point that all three of these sets of theories reflect facets of human reality; none is wholly right and none is wholly wrong. In some respects human beings do behave as machines—performing repetitive, routine, mechanistic tasks, such as operating certain kinds of equipment. The behaviorist strategies are appropriate in helping one learn to perform these tasks. Other performances are essentially operations of the brain—thinking, storing and retrieving information, solving problems. Here the strategies of the cognitive theorists are appropriate. But probably the largest number of performances in life are as living, growing organisms—performing complex and changing life roles. Here the strategies of the humanistic theorists are most appropriate.

I now felt secure about proceeding to write the book for Len Nadler explaining the relevance of learning theory for HRD practitioners. The organizing framework for the book was a continuum of different types of learning situations, as portrayed in Figure 1, with two criteria for identifying the appropriate theoretical model: complexity of the learning task (the vertical axis) and level of the learner's learning ability (the horizontal axis).

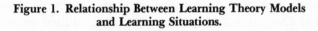

Figure 1. Relationship Between Learning Theory Models
and Learning Situations.

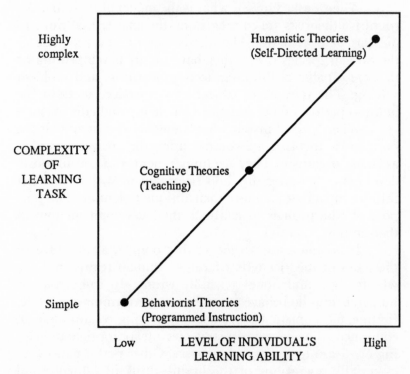

I need to make one thing clear about the meaning of "level of learning ability." Certainly general intelligence is part of it, but I think it also includes previous exposure to the subject matter, readiness to learn, motivation, and perhaps other factors. And I'd like to illustrate how I see this model working in an HRD program. If the operation to be learned is fairly simple (such as operating a simple machine) and the learner's level of learning ability is fairly low, then the behaviorists are in touch with that reality, and programmed instruction, linear computer-assisted instruction, behavior modification, and drill are appropriate strategies. If the learning task is fairly complex (such as gaining knowledge and understanding of the theory behind the operation of the machine), then the cognitive theorists are in touch with that reality, and didactic teaching is appropriate. If the learning task is highly complex (such as learning to become a more effective manager) and the level of the learner's learning ability is high, the humanistic theorists are in touch with that reality, and self-directed learning projects are appropriate.

I finished the manuscript and mailed it to Len Nadler on September 7, 1972, just two weeks after the target date. The editors of Gulf Publishing thought the working title "Learning Theory and Human Resources Development" did not describe what the book is really about, so they changed the title to *The Adult Learner: A Neglected Species*. It was published in February 1973.

Learning About Meaningful Evaluation

During my early days in adult education, first with the National Youth Administration of Massachusetts and then as director of adult education at the YMCAs of Boston and Chicago, I relied on what we would now call "informal subjective data" to evaluate how well our programs were accomplishing their objectives. In retrospect, I realize how skillful I and my fellow adult educators of that era had become in eliciting information from participants in our programs about what outcomes were being achieved. By talking with the participants in informal settings—cafeterias, hallways, and advisory committee meetings—I was able to gather useful and objective information that caused me to make modifications in our programs.

Then, in 1944, I went away to the wars as an ensign and, later, a lieutenant (junior grade) in the U.S. Navy. When I returned in 1946 and enrolled in the School of Education at the University of Chicago, it was like landing on a strange new planet. While I was away, the statisticians had taken over. The dominant note in evaluation had become quantification. Unless an evaluation report was stated in numbers, it wasn't respectable. I jumped aboard that bandwagon, took my quota of required courses in statistics and educational measurement, and became proficient in constructing pretests and posttests, rating scales, and the like and in testing the significance of differences by t-tests, chi square, and other statistical techniques that I have long since forgotten.

Around the middle of the 1970s I began asking myself what I learned from the quantitative data I had been collecting for years, and I couldn't think of much. In 1978 there appeared a book by Michael Q. Patton, *Utilization-Focused Evaluation*, that started giving me some clues as to why this was so. Patton, who was director of the Minnesota Center for Social Research at the University of Minnesota, had been doing evaluation studies for many years for federally funded educational and human services projects. In the mid-seventies he began wondering why so many recommendations he made in his studies were not being implemented by the projects. He interviewed a number of the project directors and policymakers and learned that the questions he was asking in his evaluation research were often not the questions the project leaders were interested in. Most strikingly, they were frequently more interested in the qualitative outcomes of their programs (How differently do the participants perform in their jobs after the training?) than in the quantitative data. So he decided that before undertaking a program evaluation he should find out what the program managers wanted to know and how they would use the information—hence, the title of the book. And he found himself more and more using qualitative evaluation methods.

But I still stuck pretty much to quantitative evaluation; I didn't really understand how to do qualitative evaluation. Then, in 1980, Patton came out with the book I had been waiting for: *Qualitative Evaluation Methods*. I began using such methods described in detail by Patton as participant observation, in-depth interviewing, diaries, and case studies. Almost immediately I began to get information that led to substantial changes in my programs and in my personal behavior. The next year Patton published a third book, *Creative Evaluation*, the main theme of which is that evaluation is a creative process in which the evaluator has to make a judgment about which methods—quantitative or qualitative—will produce the kind of data required for a particular situation. This was followed in 1982 by a fourth book, *Practical Evaluation,* in which Patton builds on the themes of the previous books and provides practical tools and procedures for reaching desired goals.

I soon discovered that Patton was not an isolated heretic in proposing this new way of thinking about evaluation. In 1980 Lee Cronbach and Associates published *Toward Reform of Program Evaluation,* and in 1981 Egon Guba and Yvonna Lincoln published *Effective Evaluation: Improving the Usefulness of Evaluation Through Responsive and Naturalistic Approaches.* Both books propose a balance between quantitative and qualitative evaluation. I perceive that in the last decade we have made a 180 degree turn in our very way of thinking about the evaluation of learning, away from an almost exclusively quantitative approach toward an increasing emphasis on a qualitative approach.

Now in my courses and workshops, instead of passing out an evaluation instrument with a numerical rating scale, I explain the "new look" in evaluation and ask the participants to do a qualitative evaluation of the course or workshop. I put them into small groups of four or five and ask them to agree on statements concerning the quality of the design, climate, techniques, and learning outcomes of the program. I ask one member of each group to volunteer to write these statements on a sheet of paper and turn the sheets in to me when we adjourn. I reproduce and analyze some of these evaluations in Chapter Six.

Learning to Make Things Happen by Releasing the Energy of Others

Several years ago I began an intellectual adventure that has paid high dividends in terms of understanding the role of leadership and in selecting more effective leadership strategies. The adventure consisted of seeing what would happen if one conceptualized a social system (family, group, organization, agency, corporation, school, college, community, state, nation, or world) as a system of human energy.

All at once a set of questions very different from those typically asked by leaders started coming to mind: What is the sum total of the human energy available in the system? What proportion of this energy is now being used? Where is the unused energy located? Why is it not being tapped? What kinds of energy (physical, intellectual, psychic, moral, artistic, technical, social) are represented? What might be done to release this energy for accomplishing greater goals for the system and the individuals in it?

By virtue of simply asking these kinds of questions I began to have to think differently about the role of leadership. Having been raised in the era of Frederick Taylor's "scientific management," I had perceived the role of leadership to consist primarily of *controlling* followers or subordinates. Effective leaders, I had been taught, were those who were able to get people to follow their orders. The consequence of this doctrine was, of course, that the output of the system was limited to the vision and ability of the leader; when I realized this fact, I started rethinking the function of leadership. It gradually came to me that the highest function of leadership is *releasing* the energy of the people in the system and managing the processes for giving that energy direction toward mutually beneficial goals.

Perhaps a better way of saying this is that *creative leadership* is that form of leadership which releases the creative energy of the people being led.

In the intervening years since this way of thinking emerged in my mind, I have been trying to understand it— and test its validity—in two ways. First, I have been observing leaders of various sorts (teachers, business executives, educational administrators, and organizational and political leaders) through this frame of reference. I have tried to see if I could identify characteristics that "releasing leaders" possess and "controlling leaders" do not. Second, I have reexamined the research literature on human behavior, organizational dynamics, and leadership to find out what support it contains for this way of viewing the concept of leadership. I would like to share with you the results of this bifocal inquiry in the form of the following propositions regarding the behavioral characteristics of creative leaders.

1. *Creative leaders make a different set of assumptions—essentially positive—about human nature from the assumptions—essentially negative—made by controlling leaders.* It has been my observation that creative leaders have faith in people, offer them challenging opportunities, and delegate responsibility to them. Two of the clearest presentations of these contrasting assumptions in the literature are reproduced in Table 1: by Douglas McGregor in the case of assumptions by managers and by Carl Rogers in the case of assumptions by educators.

The validity of the positive set of assumptions is supported by research which indicates that when people perceive the locus of control to reside within themselves, they are more creative and productive (Lefcourt, 1976) and that the more they feel their unique potential is being utilized, the greater their achievement (Herzberg, Mausner, and Snyderman, 1959; Herzberg, 1966; Maslow, 1970).

2. *Creative leaders accept as a law of human nature that people feel a commitment to a decision in proportion to the extent that they feel they have participated in making it.* Creative leaders, therefore, involve their clients, workers, or students in every step of the planning process, assessing needs, formulating goals, designing lines of action, carrying out activities, and evaluating results (except, perhaps, in emergencies). The validity of this proposition is supported by locus of control studies (Lefcourt, 1976) and by research on organizational change (Bennis, Benne, and Chin, 1968; Greiner, 1971; Lippitt, 1969; Martorana and Kuhns, 1975), administration (Baldridge, Curtis, Ecker, and Riley, 1978; Dykes, 1968; Getzels, Lipham, and Campbell, 1968; Likert, 1967; McGregor, 1967), decision making (Marrow, Bowers, and Seashore, 1968; Millett, 1968; Simon, 1961), and organizational dynamics (Argyris, 1962; Etzioni, 1961; Schein and Bennis, 1965; Zander, 1977).

3. *Creative leaders believe in and use the power of self-fulfilling prophecy.* They understand that people tend to come

Table 1. A Comparison of Assumptions About Human Nature
and Behavior by Leaders in Management and Education.

Theory X Assumptions About Human Nature (McGregor) (Controlling)	*Assumptions Implicit in Current Education (Rogers) (Controlling)*
The average human being inherently dislikes work and will avoid it if he can.	The student cannot be trusted to pursue his or her own learning.
Because of this characteristically human dislike of work, most people must be coerced, controlled, threatened in the interest of organizational objectives.	Presentation equals learning. The aim of education is to accumulate brick upon brick of factual knowledge.
The average human being prefers to be directed, wishes to avoid responsibility, has relatively little ambition, wants security above all.	The truth is known. Creative citizens develop from passive learners. Evaluation is education and education is evaluation.

Theory Y Assumptions About Human Nature (Releasing)	*Assumptions Relevant to Significant Experiential Learning (Releasing)*
The expenditure of physical and mental effort is as natural as play or rest.	Human beings have a natural potentiality for learning.
External control and threat of punishment are not the only means for bringing about effort toward organizational objectives. Man will exercise self-direction and self-control in the service of objectives to which he is committed.	Significant learning takes place when the subject matter is perceived by the student as relevant to his or her own purposes. Much significant learning is acquired through doing.
Commitment to objectives is a function of the rewards associated with their achievement.	Learning is facilitated by students' responsible participation in the learning process.
The average human being learns, under proper conditions, not only to accept but to seek responsibility.	Self-initiated learning involving the whole person—feelings as well as intellect—is the most pervasive and lasting.
A high capacity for imagination, ingenuity, and creativity in solving organizational problems is widely, not narrowly distributed in the population.	Creativity in learning is best facilitated when self-criticism and self-evaluation are primary, and evaluation by others is of secondary importance.

Table 1. A Comparison of Assumptions About Human Nature
and Behavior by Leaders in Management and Education, Cont'd.

Theory Y Assumptions About Human Nature (Releasing)	Assumptions Relevant to Significant Experiential Learning (Releasing)
Under the conditions of modern industrial life, the intellectual potential of the average human being is only partially utilized.	The most socially useful thing to learn in the modern world is the process of learning, a continuing openness to experience, an incorporation into oneself of the process of change.

Source: Adapted from McGregor, 1960, pp. 33–34 and 47–48, and
from Rogers, 1980, pp. 294–301, as presented in Knowles, 1984, p. 108.

up to other people's expectations for them. The creative coach
conveys to the team that he or she knows they are capable
of winning; the good supervisor's employees know that he
or she has faith that they will do superior work; the good
teacher's students are convinced that they are the best students
in school. The classic study demonstrating this principle,
Rosenthal and Jacobson's *Pygmalion in the Classroom* (1968),
showed that the students of teachers who were told that they
were superior students *were* superior students whereas the students of teachers who were told that they were inferior students *were* inferior students. And, of course, there was no
difference in the natural ability of the two groups of students.
The relationship between positive self-concept and superior
performance has been demonstrated in studies of students
(Chickering, 1969; Felker, 1974; Rogers, 1969; Tough, 1979)
and of general life achievement (Adams-Webber, 1979; Coan,
1974; Gale, 1974; Kelly, 1955; Loevinger, 1976; McClelland,
1975).

4. *Creative leaders highly value individuality.* They
sense that people perform at a higher level when they are
operating on the basis of their unique strengths, talents, interests, and goals than when they are trying to conform to some
imposed stereotype. They are comfortable with a pluralistic
culture and tend to be bored with one that is monolithic. As
managers, they encourage a team arrangement in which each

member works at what he or she does best and enjoys most;
as teachers, they strive to tailor the learning strategies to fit
the individual learning styles, paces, starting points, needs,
and interests of all the students. This proposition is widely
supported in the research literature (Combs and Snygg, 1959;
Csikszentmihalyi, 1975; Erikson, 1974; Goldstein and Blackman, 1978; Gowan, Demos, and Torrance, 1967; Kagan and
Moss, 1962; Maslow, 1970; Messick and Associates, 1976;
Moustakas, 1974; Tyler, 1978).

I would like to add another dimension to this proposition—more of a philosophical note than a behavioral observation. It is that creative leaders probably have a different sense
of the purpose of life from that of controlling leaders. Creative
leaders see the purpose of all life activities—work, learning,
recreation, civic participation, worship—to be to enable each
individual to achieve his or her full and unique potential.
They seek to help each person become what Maslow (1970)
calls a self-actualizing person. The controlling leader's mission, on the other hand, is to produce conforming people.

5. *Creative leaders stimulate and reward creativity.*
They understand that in a world of accelerating change, creativity is a basic requirement for the survival of individuals,
organizations, and societies. They exemplify creativity in
their own behavior and provide an environment that encourages and rewards innovation in others. They make it
legitimate for people to experiment, and treat failures as
opportunities to learn rather than as acts to be punished (Barron, 1963; Bennis, 1966; Cross, 1976; Davis and Scott, 1971;
Gardner, 1963; Gowan, Demos, and Torrance, 1967; Herzberg,
1966; Ingalls, 1976; Kagan and Moss, 1962; Schön, 1971;
Toffler, 1980; Zahn, 1966).

6. *Creative leaders are committed to a process of continuous change and are skillful in managing change.* They
understand the difference between static and innovative organizations, as portrayed in Table 2, and aspire to make their
organizations the latter. They are well grounded in the theory
of change and skillful in selecting the most effective strategies
for bringing about change (Arends and Arends, 1977; Bal-

Table 2. Some Characteristics of Static Versus Innovative Organizations.

Dimensions	Characteristics	
	Static Organizations	Innovative Organizations
Structure	Rigid—much energy given to maintaining permanent departments, committees; reverence for tradition, constitution and bylaws. Hierarchical—adherence to chain of command. Roles defined narrowly. Property bound.	Flexible—much use of temporary task forces; easy shifting of departmental lines; readiness to change constitution, depart from tradition. Multiple linkages based on functional collaboration. Roles defined broadly. Property mobile.
Atmosphere	Task centered, impersonal. Cold, formal, reserved. Suspicious.	People centered, caring. Warm, informal, intimate. Trusting.
Management Philosophy and Attitudes	Function of management is to control personnel through coercive power. Cautious—low risk taking. Attitude toward errors: to be avoided. Emphasis on personnel selection. Self-sufficiency—closed system regarding sharing resources. Low tolerance for ambiguity.	Function of management is to release the energy of personnel; power is used supportively. Experimental—high risk taking. Attitude toward errors: to be learned from. Emphasis on personal development. Interdependency—open system regarding sharing resources. High tolerance for ambiguity.
Decision Making and Policy-Making	High participation at top, low at bottom. Clear distinction between policy-making and policy execution. Decision making by legal mechanisms. Decisions treated as final.	Relevant participation by all those affected. Collaborative policy-making and policy execution. Decision making by problem solving. Decisions treated as hypotheses to be tested.
Communication	Restricted flow—constipated. One-way—downward. Feelings repressed or hidden.	Open flow—easy access. Multidirectional—up, down, sideways. Feelings expressed.

Source: Knowles, 1984, p. 100.

dridge and Deal, 1975; Bennis, Benne, and Chin, 1968; Goodlad, 1975; Greiner, 1971; Hefferlin, 1969; Hornstein, 1971; Lippitt, 1978; Martorana and Kuhns, 1975; Schein and Bennis,
1965; Tedeschi, 1972; Zurcher, 1977).

7. *Creative leaders emphasize internal motivators over
external motivators.* They understand the distinction revealed
in Herzberg's (1966) research between satisfiers (motivators)—
such as achievement, recognition, fulfilling work, responsibility, advancement, and growth—and dissatisfiers (hygienic
factors)—such as organizational policy and administration,
supervision, working conditions, interpersonal relations, salary, status, and job security. Creative leaders take steps to
reduce the dissatisfiers but concentrate their energy on optimizing the satisfiers. This position is strongly supported by
subsequent research (Levinson and Price, 1963; Likert, 1967).

8. *Creative leaders encourage people to be self-directing.*
They sense intuitively what researchers have been telling us
for some time—that a universal characteristic of the maturation process is movement from a state of dependency toward
states of increasing self-directedness (Baltes, 1978; Erikson,
1959, 1964, 1974; Goulet and Baltes, 1970; Gubrium and Buckholdt, 1977; Havighurst, 1970; Kagan and Moss, 1962; Loevinger, 1976; Rogers, 1969). They realize that because of previous
conditioning as dependent learners in their school experience,
adults need initial help in learning to be self-directing and
look to leaders for this kind of help (Kidd, 1973; Knowles,
1975, 1977, 1980; Tough, 1967, 1979). And to provide this
kind of help, they have developed their skills as facilitators
and consultants to a high level (Bell and Nadler, 1985; Blake
and Mouton, 1976; Bullmer, 1975; Carkhuff, 1969; Combs,
Avila, and Purkey, 1978; Lippitt and Lippitt, 1978; Laughary
and Ripley, 1979; Pollack, 1976; Schein, 1969; Schlossberg
and Troll, 1978).

No doubt additional propositions and behavioral characteristics could be identified, but these are the ones that stand
out in my observation of creative leaders and review of the
literature as being most central. I have seen wonderful things
happen when they have been put into practice. I have seen

low-achieving students become high-achieving students when they discovered the excitement of self-directed learning under the influence of a creative teacher. I have seen bench workers in a factory increase their productivity and get a new sense of personal pride and fulfillment under a creative supervisor. I have seen an entire college faculty become creative facilitators of learning and content resource consultants through the stimulation of a creative administration. And I have observed several instances in which the line managers of major corporations moved from controlling managers to releasing managers when their management-development programs were geared to these propositions.

Perhaps we are on the verge of beginning to understand how to optimize the release of the enormous pent-up energy in our human energy systems.

Chapter 3

Landmarks and Heroes
in Adult Education

My academic discipline is history. So whenever I enter into a new field of endeavor, my instinctive impulse is to find out whatever I can about its historical background. Also, one of the ingredients of a social system's culture is its heroes—people who serve as role models for the culture (Deal and Kennedy, 1982). As a new participant in the adult education movement in this country, I wanted to find out who its heroes were. This chapter reflects those landmarks and heroes with most meaning to me.

When I discovered in the mid 1930s (see Chapter One) that I was operating in the field of adult education, I undertook to discover if it had a history. The contemporary books I first examined seemed to place its roots in programs to "Americanize" the waves of immigrants flooding this country around the turn of this century. I therefore assumed that I was a part of a relatively new social invention.

Really Ancient Roots

I participated in a seminar led by Cyril Houle at the University of Chicago and learned that, lo and behold, the education of adults was probably the earliest form of systematic education. I learned, in fact, that all of the great teachers of ancient times—Confucius and Lao-tsu in ancient China; the

Hebrew prophets and Jesus in biblical times; Aristotle, Plato, Socrates, and other ancient Greeks; and Cicero, Euclid, and other ancient Roman teachers—taught adults, not children.

Because their experience was with adults, they came to have a very different concept of the learning-teaching process than later came to dominate formal education, I discovered. They recognized that adults enter into an educational activity with a wealth of experience that influences what they want to learn and that is itself a rich resource for one another's learning. They also perceived learning to be a process of active inquiry, not passive reception of transmitted content.

Accordingly, they invented techniques for engaging learners in active inquiry. The ancient Chinese and Hebrews invented what we would now call the case method or critical incident, in which the leader or one of the group members would describe a problem situation, often in the form of a parable, and jointly they would explore its characteristics and possible resolutions. The Greeks invented what we now call the Socratic dialogue, in which the leader or a group member would pose a question or a dilemma and the group would pool their thinking and experience in seeking an answer or a solution. The Romans were more confrontational: they used challenges that forced group members to state positions and then defend them.

I now realize that those early footprints in the sands of adult education's time were amazingly congruent with modern concepts of adult learning as portrayed in the andragogical model. I keep being puzzled at how many centuries it took for our field to catch up with its beginnings! The ancient teachers were following their intuitions rather than some prescribed doctrine such as pedagogy. And I began to realize that this is what I had been doing, too, and I felt reinforced.

The Middle Ages and Renaissance

As in the case of most aspects of historical development, there is a comparative void in the literature about adult education between the fall of Rome and the Renaissance. The main footprint left during this period, as I see it, was the institutionalization of education for children. Between the seventh and twelfth centuries schools were established in cathedrals and monasteries in Europe primarily for the preparation of young boys for the priesthood. As a result of the teachers in these schools having as their principal mission the indoctrination of young boys in the beliefs, faith, and rituals of the Catholic Church, they evolved a set of assumptions about learning and strategies for teaching that came to be subsumed under the label "pedagogy," literally meaning "the art and science of teaching children." When public schools started being organized several centuries later, this pedagogical model was the only model teachers knew about (apparently few of them read Plato), and so our whole international system of elementary, secondary, and higher education became frozen into that model.

The Renaissance, between the fourteenth and seventeenth centuries, was marked by a flowering of the arts and literature and by the beginnings of modern science. But it seemed to me that its two footprints that had the greatest impact on the advancement of adult education were the invention of the printing press and the Protestant Reformation in the sixteenth century, when it became a standard expectation that people would continue their religious education by reading the Bible and other printed materials.

Modern Footprints

During the three centuries following the Renaissance a number of new institutional forms expressly for the education of adults evolved in Europe: the folk high schools in Germany, the Netherlands, and the Scandinavian countries; the workers' education movement in Great Britain; and study circles of a variety of types in many countries. Some attempts were made to transplant some of these forms to the United States, but with limited durability. Americans seemed to have a penchant for creating their own forms.

Early institutional forms of adult learning that emerged in our own country during the colonial period were apprenticeship, private vocational schools, subscription libraries, church-sponsored educational programs, museums, town meetings, and agricultural societies. But probably every adult educator's first American hero is Benjamin Franklin. He was our first visible role model of the concept that learning is a lifelong process. He founded the first uniquely American adult education institution: the Junto, a discussion club organized by Franklin and eleven cronies in 1727 to explore such intellectual challenges as morals, politics, and natural philosophy. He was also instrumental in founding the American Philosophical Society, the Franklin Institute of Philadelphia, the University of Pennsylvania, and the first American public library. Through his writings and by the example of his life he deeply ingrained into the American stream of thought a compulsion toward self-improvement that has exerted a dominant influence on the American attitude toward continuing education. He was, in my estimation, our first patron saint of adult education. The Junto was a model for a variety of discussion groups, study circles, and other voluntary organizations that emerged in subsequent decades under a variety of auspices. Its special significance to me is that it set the tone of voluntarism that has been such a powerful force in American adult education.

This tendency toward citizen involvement intensified as the colonists moved toward rebellion from colonial status, and an awareness began to emerge that self-government would require an informed citizenry. There was a rising flood of letters of correspondence (which I think we would now call "networking"), pamphlets, editorials, speeches, poems, and plays that explored the concepts, issues, and strategies of creating a democratic society.

Between the Revolution and the Civil War the United States emerged as an independent, self-governing nation and took on characteristics that further set it apart from its European antecedents. This period marked the beginning of the Industrial Revolution and the rapid growth of commerce that brought on an upsurge of secular thought and interest in natural science that produced almost a compulsion for knowledge. A pioneering attempt to satisfy this compulsion was made by Professor Benjamin Silliman of Yale College. In 1830 Professor Silliman gave a course of popular lectures on natural science for the benefit of a class of ladies and gentlemen in New Haven. It proved so popular that he began to lecture outside of New Haven, in Hartford, Lowell, Salem, and Boston. By 1859 Silliman's lectures had been extended south and west to Pittsburgh, Baltimore, Mobile, Natchez, and St. Louis. Thus was sown the seed of a major new institutional form of adult education, university extension, which flowered half a century later.

At about the same time Josiah Holbrook of Derby, Connecticut, created another uniquely American institutional form of adult education—the American Lyceum. His idea was to form a national network of local study groups that would reach every part of the nation. He proceeded to demonstrate that his plan would work by personally organizing the first town lyceum in Millbury, Massachusetts, in 1826, and ten more lyceums in neighboring towns the next year. By 1828 there were around one hundred lyceums in local towns and counties. The movement continued to spread and by 1835 there were about three thousand town lyceums, more than a hundred county lyceums, and fifteen state lyceums. Lyceum meetings had two purposes: self-improvement of their members through lectures and discussions on science, history, and social issues, and promotion of the idea of tax-supported public schools. By the early 1840s the mission of promoting public schools had been largely accomplished, and the national lyceum system gradually disintegrated into a series of local lecture series. But the lyceum movement left several permanent deposits in the mainstream of American culture and, particularly, of adult education. It spawned the idea of an integrated national system of local groups with an adult educational purpose. Its experience in this regard no doubt influenced the later development of such organizations as women's clubs, service clubs, parent-teacher associations, and the Great

Books program. It developed an educational technique, the lecture forum, that was later to be adopted and extended by such successors as Chautauqua, university extension, and Town Meeting of the Air. Its publication of scientific tracts for home study foreshadowed the correspondence course. Perhaps, it even suggested the idea of a national movement for the advancement of adult education. Josiah Holbrook was, indeed, an innovative and visionary hero.

Other institutional forms that emerged during the first half of the nineteenth century included mechanics' and mercantile libraries and institutes, the Lowell Institute in Boston and the Cooper Union in New York, public libraries, myriad voluntary organizations, and evening schools. This American penchant to form voluntary associations to provide community services caused the great French observer Alexis de Tocqueville to note in 1831 that "Wherever at the head of some new undertaking you see the government in France, or a man of rank in England, in the United States you will be sure to find an association" (Tocqueville, [1835] 1954, p. 114).

A landmark of this period that was to have an enormous effect on the shaping of adult education was the passage in 1862 of the Land Grant Act under the sponsorship of another hero—Senator Morrill of Vermont (and, therefore, widely known as the Morrill Act). This act set aside vast acres of land in every state for the establishment of a land-grant college for research and study in the agricultural and mechanical arts by average students—truly a people's university. This was the foundation onto which fifty years later one of the largest and most impactful programs of adult education—the Cooperative Extension Service—would be grafted.

The founding of Chautauqua Institution on the shores of Chautauqua Lake in western New York in 1874 by Dr. John Vincent, secretary of the Methodist Sunday School Union, and Lewis Miller, a businessman and church layman, turned out to be a heroic act. Initially conceived as a pandenominational normal school for Sunday school teachers, it proved to be so popular that it attracted participants other than Sunday school teachers and its program was broadened to include every aspect of culture. In 1878 the first integrated core program of adult education, the Chautauqua Literary and Scientific Circle, was established by these two visionaries. The C.L.S.C. was a four-year program of home reading in history and literature carried on in connection with local reading circles. Diplomas were awarded for the successful completion of four years of study and discussion. In the next few years Chautauqua added summer schools in languages, liberal arts, speech, physical education, music, domestic science, and library training. The summer schools attracted outstanding educators to their faculties and achieved high academic recognition. It also expanded its informal program, with numerous lecture series, classes, and conferences on pressing national economic, political, social, theological, and international issues. What became known as the "Chautauqua Circuit" brought both entertainment and culture to rural America. Chautauqua, to this day a thriving adult education institution, is assured a place in history by the influence it has had on the lives of thousands of individuals. But it merits additional credit for the contributions it has made to the adult educational field at large. It pioneered the development of such new forms and methods as the correspondence course, summer school, university extension, and book clubs, which have been adopted by colleges and universities, public schools, and myriad voluntary and commercial organizations.

Another hero of this era was William Rainey Harper, a professor of Hebrew at Yale, who offered the first correspondence course at Chautauqua in 1879. The experiment, at first an informal "advice by mail" process, proved so popular that by 1883 several courses with regular assignments were offered under several instructors. The success of the home-study program at Chautauqua inspired Dr. Harper, when he became president of the University of Chicago in 1892, to establish an extension department, with a correspondence division, in the new university. This innovation in higher education later came to be adopted by many universities across the country.

Two heroes of the American public library movement of this era stand out above many others. One was Andrew

Carnegie, who between 1881 and 1917 contributed over $41 million to the building of community libraries. While the public library movement had been expanding under its own steam up until that time, most of the libraries were located in large cities. Carnegie's financing of library buildings made it possible for most towns and counties in the country to have their own libraries. The other hero was Melvil Dewey, the chief librarian at Columbia University. In addition to devising the standard decimal system of book classification that has made books more accessible to succeeding generations, he was instrumental in persuading the regents of the University of the State of New York in 1891 to appropriate $10,000 for the organization of university extension in that state.

The one component of the adult education movement that has probably had the greatest impact on the quality of life in this country is agricultural education. Starting in the early nineteenth century local and regional agricultural societies and agricultural fairs exposed farmers to improved practices that steadily increased the productivity of our farms. In the last quarter of the century national voluntary organizations, such as the Grange, the Farmers' Union, and the American Farm Bureau Federation, carried on and extended this mission. Many unsung heroes were involved in this achievement, but the hero who stands out above all others, in my estimation, was Seaman A. Knapp, who invented a method that proved to be more effective than any yet known for causing farmers to change their practices. Knapp had observed that farmers did not change their practices readily as a result of merely being informed about better farming practices. He reasoned that if they actually tried out new methods on their own farms and experienced superior results, they would quickly adopt the more effective methods. His invention of the results-demonstration method proved to be one of the most effective methods in the adult educational arsenal, and it has been adapted in many other fields of endeavor. The success of his work was influential in the passage of the Smith-Lever Act in 1914, which established the Cooperative Extension Service, combining the resources of federal, state, and county agricultural agencies in providing educational services not only in regard to farming practices but also in home economics and youth work.

Two heroes from Wisconsin stand out in the establishment of the university extension movement in this country: Charles R. Van Hise and Louis E. Reber. Although extension lectures and courses had proliferated in the last quarter of the nineteenth century and extension departments had been established at the University of Wisconsin and the University of Kansas in 1891 and at the University of Chicago in 1892, the movement failed to gain much momentum until these two heroes invigorated it. In his inaugural address in 1904 as president of the University of Wisconsin, Van Hise set the stage for a new era by proposing that the university should extend its scope until all areas of knowledge were covered, from agriculture to the fine arts, and the university's campus was defined by the boundaries of the state. In 1907 the extension division of the University of Wisconsin was reorganized by Dean Reber, and a new spirit was infused into the idea of extension by shifting from an emphasis on academic subjects toward an all-embracing concept of the role of the university in serving all of the people of the state in relation to the full scope of life concerns, including the agricultural, political, social, and moral. Extension divisions were rapidly established in other universities. The founding of the National University Extension Association in 1915 stands as a symbol of the recognition of general extension as a permanent element in our national system of higher education.

The dominant theme in the period between the Civil War and World War I, as I see it, was "multiplication." The period opened with hundreds of activities for the education of adults and closed with thousands. A number of new institutional forms of adult education were either created or became firmly established, including correspondence schools, summer schools, university extension, residential labor colleges, evening schools, health education organizations, religious education societies, agricultural societies, parks and recreation centers, and a wide variety of national voluntary organizations.

A few new methods were invented: the demonstration method pioneered by the Cooperative Extension Service, the noncredit short course, the home-study course, the knowledge-sharing conference, the short-term institute, group discussion, and visual aids. The general character of the content of adult learning shifted from general knowledge to several pinpointed areas of focus: vocational education, citizenship education, women's education, public affairs forums, leisure-time activities, and health education. These footprints were clearly in tune, it seems to me, with the needs of this era of industrialization, immigration, emancipation, urbanization, and national maturation.

This period also witnessed increasing participation by government in the development of adult educational opportunities. At the federal level this trend was evidenced by the establishment of the Department of Education, which eventually added an office of adult education specialist; the passage of the Smith-Lever Act creating the Cooperative Extension Service; and the passage of the Smith-Hughes Vocational Education Act, which spawned the founding of vocational schools open to adults around the country. At the state level this trend was evidenced by the passage of permissive legislation authorizing school systems to serve adults in a number of states, the provision of direct financial aid for adult classes in a few states, and the establishment of adult education bureaus in the departments of education in several states. At the local level the trend was evidenced by increasing support for evening schools, libraries, museums, and county agricultural extension services. Adult education was still perceived as a "second-class citizen" in the national educational enterprise, but the footprints it was leaving were leading somewhere.

The period since World War I has been an era of continuous and rapid expansion in the number of institutions offering adult educational opportunities and the number of adults participating. But it has also witnessed the shaping of adult education into a coherent and increasingly prestigious field of study and practice. The founding of the Department of Immigrant Education (later changed to Adult Education) in the National Education Association in 1921 signaled the recognition of adult education as an integral function of the public schools and the rising awareness of adult education as an emerging profession. The founding of national membership organizations—the American Association for Adult Education in 1926 and its successors, the Adult Education Association of the U.S.A. in 1951 and the American Association for Adult and Continuing Education in 1982—gave the adult education movement a national identity and its members an organizational home.

In fact, if any one person is entitled to be known as the father of the adult education movement in this country, my nominee is Frederick K. Keppel. When he came to the presidency of the Carnegie Corporation of New York in 1923, one of his first acts was to persuade the trustees to include adult education and the arts in their list of interests, which until then had consisted of education at the college and university level, research (especially medical), and libraries. Keppel had been impressed by adult educational developments in Europe following World War I, and he was disturbed that so little information existed about adult education in the United States. Between November 1925 and March 1926, he convened four regional meetings of adult education workers from a variety of agencies to obtain facts about what educational services were being offered to adults and to solicit opinions as to what would be required to develop a strong adult education movement in this country. The principal outcome of these meetings was the formation of the American Association for Adult Education at a conference held in Chicago on March 26 and 27, 1926. In my view, this event marked the beginning of an organized adult education movement in the United States.

It would be impossible to name Frederick Keppel as a hero without tying in the name of Morse A. Cartwright, his assistant at the Carnegie Corporation, who became the first executive director of the American Association for Adult Education. Serving in that capacity for twenty-three years (1926–1949), Cartwright was the strategic leader and policy shaper of the new association. By involving many of the intellectual lights of the time, such as James E. Russell, Newton D. Baker, Felix M. Warburg, Dorothy Canfield Fisher, Edward L. Thorndike, Charles A. Beard, Everett Dean Martin, William Allen Nielson, Alvin Johnson, Harry A. Overstreet, Alexander Meiklejohn, Lyman Bryson, and Alain Leroy Locke, in both leadership positions (all of the above were presidents of the association) and publications, he was instrumental in bringing intellectual respectability to the association and the emerging adult education movement.

The establishment of graduate degree programs in adult education, first at Teachers College, Columbia University, in 1932, and their eventual spread to more than a hundred universities have given adult education a sense of professional identity and a growing body of research-based knowledge about adult learners and adult learning.

The most notable expansion of institutional offerings in recent years, in my view, has been in business and industry, community colleges, government agencies, mass media, and professional societies. It has become a widely accepted notion that all organizations have as their mission not only the production of goods or the delivery of services but the continuing personal and professional development of their employees, members, and clients, as well. In fact, it has become increasingly difficult to distinguish "adult education institutions" as separate entities. I now perceive that almost all societal institutions are engaged in some way in the education of adults.

The new methods developed during the modern era have been principally in the use of electronic media: teleconferencing, television, computer-based instruction, interactive video discs, films, and multimedia learning modules. But older methods, especially forms of group discussion and experiential learning, have been refined and enriched. A strong theme running through contemporary methodology is involvement of the learners in taking responsibility for their own learning; self-directed learning has become a purple phrase in our literature.

During the last sixty-eight years, under the stimulus of two world wars, a great depression, and a rapidly accelerating pace of change in technological, political, and cultural affairs, adult education has become an integral part of the American way of life. Indeed, it has become the largest segment of our national educational enterprise. The most regrettable blemish on this otherwise noteworthy record is the fact that almost one-fifth of our adult citizens are still functionally illiterate. This, I believe, is our biggest challenge for the era ahead. We cannot afford to enter the twenty-first century with this millstone around our neck.

In Chapter One I identify the contemporary heroes who have influenced my life and career. I feel eternally grateful to these and many more unsung heroes who have contributed to both my personal and professional development and to that of the adult education movement in general. And I salute the scores of young heroes who are beginning to shape our movement for a new era, especially through their contributions in research and theory.

As I reflect on what I have learned about the historical development of adult education, I realize that this knowledge has had several effects on me as a person and as a professional adult educator. In the first place, it has given me a sense of historical perspective. I now see myself as a part of a long stream of events, ideas, and evolving institutional forms. I am not a Johnny-come-lately. I have roots that go way back in time. This realization, in turn, gives me a sense of increased stature. I belong not just to the contemporary scene; I am part of a long and significant historical movement. And this, in turn, gives me a sense of pride. An adult educator is someone who is important in the eyes of history. I am proud to be an adult educator. I don't have to apologize to anyone for the vocation I have chosen. I, too, am leaving a small footprint in the sands of time.

Chapter 4

How My Ideas About Adult Learning Have Evolved and Changed

Early Influences

As I say in Chapter One, I began sensing early in my experience (as director of related training in the National Youth Administration for Massachusetts from 1935 to 1940 and director of adult education in the YMCAs of Boston and Chicago from 1940 to 1951) that there was something different about adults as learners than I had experienced with youth as learners. I became curious about what was known about adult learners and started reading everything I could lay my hands on. Shortly after I had started at the NYA in 1935, I read Eduard Lindeman's (1926) *The Meaning of Adult Education* and was inspired by such statements as the following:

> In what areas do most people appear to find life's meaning? We have only one pragmatic guide: meaning must reside in the things for which people strive, the goals which they set for themselves, their wants, needs, desires, and wishes [p. 13].
>
> I am conceiving adult education in terms of a new technique for learning. . . . It represents a process by which the adult learns to become aware

73

of and to evaluate his experience. To do this he
cannot begin by studying "subjects" in the hope
that some day this information will be useful.
On the contrary, he begins by giving attention
to situations in which he finds himself, to problems which include obstacles to his self-fulfill-
ment. . . . In this process the teacher finds a new
function. He is no longer the oracle who speaks
from the platform of authority, but rather the
guide, the pointer-outer who also participates in
learning in proportion to the vitality and rele-
vancy of his facts and experiences. In short, my
conception of adult education is this: a cooperative venture in nonauthoritarian, informal learning, the chief purpose of which is to discover the
meaning of experience; a quest of the mind which
digs down to the roots of the preconceptions
which formulate our conduct; a technique of
learning for adults which makes education coter-
minous with life and hence elevates living itself to
the level of adventurous experiment [p. 160].

I began to understand why the young adult students in
my NYA program seemed to learn better when they participated in assessing their own needs and defining their goals,
when they were actively involved in setting course objectives
and choosing methods and resources for meeting them, when
their varied experiences were used as a resource for one
another's learning (Lindeman was an advocate of group discussion), and when the learning experiences were organized
around their life tasks or problems. Four foundation stones
for a theory of adult learning were now laid.

That same year I read Edward L. Thorndike's (1928)
Adult Learning and got research-based support for the proposition that adults could learn. (Friends of mine who were at
the 1928 annual conference of the American Association for
Adult Education at which Thorndike presented his findings
told me that when he concluded his report, the audience rose

and applauded and whistled, for they had been working in an environment where the prevailing assumption was that "You can't teach an old dog new tricks.")

In 1937 a book appeared by Dorothy Hewitt and Kirtley Mather (1937), *Adult Education: A Dynamic for Democracy*, that both deepened my appreciation of the importance of adult education (to save democracy) and gave me practical guidelines for conducting group discussion and other participatory methods. Another book that further extended my commitment to and understanding of the discussion method was Arthur D. Sheffield's (1936) *Creative Discussion*.

About a decade later three books appeared that made important contributions to my theory-seeking endeavors. Nathaniel Cantor's (1946) *Dynamics of Learning* deepened my understanding of the concepts of learner-centered education and learners' ego involvement. John Dewey's (1947) *Experience and Education* gave me a theoretical justification for emphasizing the role of learners' experience in learning. Kurt Lewin's (1948) *Resolving Social Conflicts* introduced me to field theory and the concept that forces in social systems operate to facilitate or inhibit learning.

Then, in 1948, when I started to explore possible topics for my master's thesis at the University of Chicago, I came up with the idea of extracting a set of principles and practices from the existing literature and from my own experience and that of other adult educators. The study identified, among other things, what I have called thirteen "Principles of Adult Teaching":

1. The students should understand and subscribe to the purposes of the course.
2. The students should want to learn.
3. There should be a friendly and informal climate in the learning situation.
4. Physical conditions should be favorable.
5. The students should participate and should accept some responsibility for the learning process.

6. Learning should be related to and should make use of the students' experience.
7. The teacher should know his subject matter.
8. The teacher should be enthusiastic about his subject and about teaching it.
9. Students should be able to learn at their own pace.
10. The student should be aware of his own progress and should have a sense of accomplishment.
11. The methods of instruction should be varied.
12. The teacher should have a sense of growth.
13. The teacher should have a flexible plan for the course [Knowles, 1950, pp. 32–35].

As I explain in Chapter Two, my master's thesis became my first book, *Informal Adult Education,* published by Association Press in 1950. It is clear from the title that I had not yet arrived at a coherent and comprehensive theory of adult learning. The closest I could come to an organizing theme was "informal." Surely this was an important component of a theory of adult learning, but it was far from its core.

In 1950 I discovered Harry A. Overstreet's (1949) *The Mature Mind* and found further reinforcement of the notion that adult learning is concerned with "linkages with life": "A mature person is not one who has come to a certain level of achievement and stopped there. He is rather a *maturing* person—one whose *linkages with life* are constantly becoming stronger and richer because his attitudes are such as to encourage their growth. . . . A mature person, for example, is not one who knows a large number of facts. Rather, he is one whose mental habits are such that he grows in knowledge and the wise use of it" (p. 43).

That same year I was introduced to Thomas Fansler's (1950) *Creative Power Through Discussion,* and my commitment to the discussion method was further deepened.

Midstream Influences

During the 1950s my energies were focused on founding and managing the Adult Education Association of the U.S.A., and I was only peripherally thinking about adult learning theory. However, I spent my vacations in 1952 and 1954 participating in the human relations training sessions of the National Training Laboratories in Bethel, Maine, and I became deeply interested in group dynamics and its implications for adult learning. I was especially impressed with the NTL's conceptualization of the role of trainer as a facilitator of the analysis of the group's here-and-now experience and the extraction from group members of insights and self-understanding and principles of effective interpersonal relations and group processes. And I did keep up my reading. From Robert Havighurst's ([1952] 1970) *Developmental Tasks and Education,* Pressey and Kuhlen's (1957) *Psychological Development Through the Life Span,* and Erik Erikson's (1959) *Identity and the Life Cycle* I was introduced to the field of developmental psychology and the notion that developmental stages during the adult years are a potent force in producing readiness to learn. Ralph Tyler's (1950) *Basic Principles of Curriculum and Instruction* gave me a basic understanding of the elements that need to be included in a curriculum theory.

In 1959 I retired from the AEA and was given a grant from the Fund for Adult Education of the Ford Foundation to edit a 1960 edition of the *Handbook of Adult Education in the United States.* One of the chapters I decided to include in the handbook was titled "Learning Theory in Adult Education," and I asked Jack R. Gibb, then director of research for the National Training Laboratories, to write it. In it he wrote, "The list below will be made in an effort to translate some of the basic principles, so often stated in terms that do not imply specific actions on the part of the adult educator, into statements that clearly imply action steps:

1. Learning must be problem-centered.
2. Learning must be experience-centered.

3. Experience must be meaningful to the learner.
4. The learner must be free to look at the experience.
5. The goals must be set and the search organized by the learner.
6. The learner must have feedback about progress toward goals" (Knowles, 1960, pp. 58–61).

Beginning to Build a Theory

Gibb's statement convinced me that a beginning foundation of a theory of adult learning was being laid and that this was indeed a worthwhile line of inquiry. When I was invited to Boston University to establish a graduate program in adult education in 1960, my deepest commitment was to work at developing a comprehensive theory of adult learning.

I started experimenting with what I perceived to be adult-oriented strategies in the hope that this would lead to theoretical insights. My first concern was with finding ways to involve the learners deeply in sharing responsibility in planning and carrying on their own learning. I discovered that they could indeed diagnose their own learning needs quite objectively given effective tools, support, and procedures. I found simulation exercises, self-diagnostic rating scales, and peer feedback groups to be useful tools. I had the learners develop learning objectives based on their self-diagnosed learning needs, and found that they came up with objectives that were very congruent with my ideas about what a course's objectives should be—but that the learners had a much deeper sense of ownership of them than if I had prescribed them. We then organized the objectives into "inquiry units" (in the place of a content outline), and I had the learners self-select themselves into teams of from two to four to take responsibility for researching the inquiry units and presenting their findings to the class. I found that the teams became excited and enthusiastic about their learning projects and that their presentations were much more creative than I could have planned. I experimented with such other strategies as self-evaluation, setting a classroom climate that was conducive to learning, and using learning contracts.

As I was beginning to evolve a theoretical framework from my own experimentation, I was getting increasing reinforcement from the literature. Houle's (1961) *The Inquiring Mind* helped me understand more deeply the meaning and theoretical underpinnings of self-directed learning. Bruner's (1966) *Toward a Theory of Instruction* introduced me to the theoretical base of discovery learning, which I discovered was what my use of inquiry teams was about.

My Introduction to Andragogy

By the mid-1960s a rough outline of a theoretical framework of adult learning had evolved in my mind, and in 1967 I had an experience that made it all come together. A Yugoslavian adult educator, Dusan Savicevic, participated in a summer session I was conducting at Boston University. At the end of it he came up to me with his eyes sparkling and said, "Malcolm, you are preaching and practicing andragogy." I replied, "Whatagogy?" because I had never heard the term before. He explained that the term had been coined by a teacher in a German grammar school, Alexander Kapp, in 1833, in journal articles explaining how differently he was dealing with adult students in his evening classes from the teenage students in his day classes. The term lay fallow until it was once more introduced by a German social scientist, Eugen Rosenstock, in 1921, but it did not yet receive general recognition. Then in 1957 a German teacher, Franz Poggeler, published a book, *Introduction into Andragogy: Basic Issues in Adult Education,* and this time the term was picked up by adult educators in Germany, Austria, the Netherlands, and Yugoslavia and used extensively in their literature. (Incidentally, Eduard Lindeman was introduced to the term in Europe and used it in two articles on workers' education in 1926 and 1927, but it did not appear in any other American publications.)

It made great sense to me to have a term that would enable us to discuss the growing body of knowledge about adult learners in parallel with the pedagogical model of childhood learning. I used it in the next article I wrote, "Androgogy, Not Pedagogy," in *Adult Leadership* in April 1968. (I did not learn that the correct spelling is *andragogy* until I corresponded with the publishers of Merriam-Webster dictionaries in 1968; Knowles, 1980, pp. 253-254.) But the first full-blown presentation of my andragogical model appeared in my *Modern Practice of Adult Education: Andragogy Versus Pedagogy* in 1970 (revised, 1980). At this point I saw the andragogical and pedagogical models of assumptions about learning as being dichotomous and antithetical: andragogy was good and pedagogy was bad; or, at best, pedagogy was for children and andragogy was for adults. Hence, the *versus* in the subtitle.

Andragogy Revised

During the next ten years I began getting reports from elementary and secondary school teachers who had been exposed to the andragogical model explaining that they had been experimenting with it in their programs and had found that children learned better under the andragogical assumptions and strategies in many situations. I also got reports from teachers of adults that they had found that the pedagogical assumptions and strategies were necessary with adults in some situations—such as when the learners were entering into totally strange new content areas or were learning to operate unfamiliar machines, especially where health and safety were involved.

So in the revised edition of *The Modern Practice of Adult Education* in 1980 the subtitle was changed to *From Pedagogy to Andragogy*. And I presented the two models as two parallel sets of assumptions about learners and learning that need to be checked out in each situation; in those situations in which the pedagogical assumptions are realistic, pedagogical strategies are appropriate, and vice versa. The problem with this solution is, I have discovered, the ideological pedagogs will do everything they can to keep learners dependent on them because this is their main psychic reward in teaching. Andragogs will accept dependency when it clearly is the reality and will meet the dependency needs through didactic instruction until the learners have built up a foundation of knowledge about the content area sufficient for them to feel confident about taking responsibility for planning and carrying out their own learning projects. It has been my experience, though, that even very pedagogical teachers are willing to start experimenting with the andragogical model once they experience what it is like to be treated as an adult learner, even in a one-day workshop, and are exposed to the assumptions, principles, and methods of the andragogical model. Moreover, when they experience the greater psychic rewards of learners becoming excited about learning, these teachers are converted.

Later Influences

My ideas about adult learning have been enriched and modified in the last few years as the result of several other influences. Freire's (1970) *Pedagogy of the Oppressed* made me aware of the importance of "consciousness-raising" as a part of the learning process. Maslow's (1970) *Motivation and Personality* gave me, in the framework of the hierarchy of human needs, a deeper understanding of the meaning of readiness to learn as well as the concept of the self-actualized person. Goulet and Baltes's (1970) *Life-Span Developmental Psychology* enlarged my vision of the developmental process during the adult years. *Learning to Be,* by Edgar Faure and others (1972), helped me put my ideas about adult learning into the perspective of lifelong learning. Neal Berte's (1975) *Individualizing Education by Learning Contracts* helped me refine and improve my use of contract learning as a strategy for enhancing self-directed learning. Kay Torshen's (1977) *The Mastery Approach to Competency-Based Education* deepened my understanding of and commitment to this reorientation to the purpose of learning, the critical importance of which I discuss in Chapter Eight.

I have also found a good deal of reinforcement and enrichment from the writings of contemporary adult educators, particularly, in addition to the ones already cited, Jerold Apps (1981), Edgar Boone and Associates (1980), Stephen

Brookfield (1986), Patricia Cross (1976, 1981), Gordon Darkenwald and Sharan Merriam (1982), Ronald Gross (1977, 1982), John Ingalls (1976), Roby Kidd (1973), Alan Knox (1977, 1986), Morris Keeton and Associates (1976), Patricia McLagan (1978), Leonard Nadler (1970, 1982), and Raymond Wlodkowski (1985).

Where I Stand Now

My current thinking about the pedagogical and andragogical models is summarized below.

Assumptions of the pedagogical model:

1. Regarding the need to know: Learners only need to know that they must learn what the teacher teaches if they want to pass and get promoted; they do not need to know how what they learn will apply to their lives.

2. Regarding the learner's self-concept: The teacher's concept of the learner is that of a dependent personality; therefore, the learner's self-concept becomes that of a dependent personality.

3. Regarding the role of experience: The learner's experience is of little worth as a resource for learning; the experience that counts is that of the teacher, the textbook writer, and the audiovisual aids producer. Therefore, transmittal techniques (lectures, assigned readings, audiovisual presentations, and the like) are the backbone of pedagogical methodology.

4. Regarding readiness to learn: Learners become ready to learn what the school requires them to learn if they want to pass and get promoted.

5. Regarding orientation to learning: Learners have a subject-centered orientation to learning; they see learning as acquiring subject-matter content. Therefore, learning experiences are organized according to subject-matter units and the logic of subject-matter content.

6. Regarding motivation: Learners are motivated to learn by extrinsic motivators—grades, the teacher's approval or disapproval, parental pressures.

Assumptions of the andragogical model:

1.   Regarding the need to know: Adults need to know why they need to learn something before undertaking to learn it. Tough (1979) found that when adults undertake to learn something on their own, they will invest considerable energy in probing into the benefits they will gain from learning it and the negative consequences of not learning it. Consequently, one of the new aphorisms in adult education is that the first task of the facilitator of learning is to help the learners become aware of the "need to know" (a process akin to Freire's consciousness-raising).

2.   Regarding the learner's self-concept: Adults have a self-concept of being responsible for their own lives (the psychological definition of *adult*). Once they have arrived at this self-concept, they develop a deep psychological need to be seen and treated by others as being capable of self-direction. They resent and resist situations in which they feel others are imposing their will on them. But this presents a problem to us in adult education: the minute adults walk into an activity labeled "education" or "training" or any of their synonyms, they hark back to their conditioning in previous school experience, put on their dunce hat of dependency, sit back, and say, "Teach me." As we have become aware of this problem, adult educators have been working at creating front-end learning experiences in which adults are helped to make the transition from dependent to self-directed learners (Knowles, 1975; Smith, 1982).

3.   Regarding the role of the learner's experience: Adults come into an educational activity with both a greater volume and a different quality of experience from youths. This difference in quantity and quality of experience has several consequences for adult education.

For one thing, it assures that in any group of adults there will be a wider range of individual differences in terms of background, learning style, motivation, needs, interests, and goals than is true in a group of youths—hence, the great emphasis being placed in adult education on individualization of learning and teaching strategies.

For another, it means that for many kinds of learning the richest resources for learning are within the learners themselves. Hence, the greater emphasis being given in adult education to experiential techniques—techniques that tap into the experience of the learners, such as group discussion, simulation exercises, problem-solving activities, case method, and laboratory methods—over transmittal techniques. Hence, too, the greater emphasis on peer-helping activities.

But the fact of greater experience also has some potentially negative effects. As we accumulate experience, we tend to develop mental habits, biases, and presuppositions that may cause us to close our minds to new ideas, fresh perceptions, and alternative ways of thinking. Accordingly, adult educators are trying to develop ways of helping adults to examine their habits and biases and open their minds to new approaches. Sensitivity training, value clarification, meditation, and dogmatism scales are among the techniques that are used to tackle this problem.

4.   Regarding readiness to learn: Adults become ready to learn those things they need to know or to be able to do in order to cope effectively with their real-life situations. An especially rich source of readiness to learn is the developmental tasks associated with moving from one developmental stage to the next. The critical implication of this assumption is the importance of timing learning experiences to coincide with those developmental tasks.

5.   Regarding orientation to learning: In contrast to children's and youths' subject-centered orientation to learning (at least in school), adults are life centered (or task centered or problem centered) in their orientation to learning. Accordingly, learning experiences in adult education are increasingly organized around life tasks or problems—for example, "Writing Better Business Letters" rather than "Composition 1."

6.   Regarding motivation to learn: While adults are responsive to some extrinsic motivators (better jobs, promotions, salary increases, and the like), the more potent motivators are intrinsic motivators (the desire for increased self-esteem, quality of life, responsibility, job satisfaction, and

the like). Tough (1979) found in his research that all normal adults are motivated to keep growing and developing, but that this motivation is frequently blocked by such barriers as negative self-concept as a student, inaccessibility of opportunities or resources, time constraints, and programs that violate principles of adult learning.

But More Changes Are Coming

This, then, is where my thinking about adult learning stands at this time. As I predict in Chapters Seven and Eight, however, we are now on the verge of some major breakthroughs in our understanding of the learning process. I am therefore certain that if this book is revised in ten years, it will report substantial changes in my thinking.

Chapter 5

Fifteen Questions
I Am Frequently Asked
and Answers I Give

As I explain a little further on, I open my workshops and courses with a climate-setting exercise, one element of which is asking the participants to pool the questions, problems, and concerns that they hope will be dealt with in the program. I'd like to share the most common and most interesting (or challenging) questions and summarize my answers.

Q. How do you motivate adults to learn? (This is without doubt the single most frequent question I get, in some form or another.)
A. Since I deal with this question in some detail in Chapter Two, in the section entitled "Overcoming Resistance to Learning," I'll simply refer you to that section.

Q. How can we achieve greater understanding of and support for our programs from policymakers and managers?
A. This also is a very common question, and I convert it to the question "How can we educate our bosses?" I explain that most executives in business and industry, governmental agencies, voluntary organizations, and even educational institutions know about learning only from what they have experienced in being taught in traditional schools and colleges. They have had little or no exposure to modern concepts of

adult learning. Therefore, I propound, adult educators and human resource development professionals have an obligation to make it clear to their bosses that they are professionals who are operating out of a distinctive body of knowledge, theory, and practice and that they are willing to share that body of knowledge with their bosses. The problem is how to do this without denigrating or threatening them. Over the course of the years a number of my former students and colleagues have described how they have gone about solving this problem successfully. Here are some of the gems.

• One of my former students, a director of human resource development in a corporation, made a survey of his executives to find out which periodicals they respected. (Note: he didn't ask which ones they read.) At the top of the list was the *Harvard Business Review*, but several other business school journals were represented, along with *Fortune*, the *Wall Street Journal*, and *Forbes*. He subscribed to these periodicals and scanned each issue for articles explaining the new look in HRD. When he found such articles, he would make copies and send them (along with appropriate reprints from *Training* and the *Training and Development Journal*) to key executives with handwritten notes saying he thought that they would find them interesting and he would be glad to chat about them over lunch. He reported that some of the articles even became the subject of discussions in executive meetings. He is convinced that corporate support for the HRD program (and its budget) improved markedly as a result of this strategy.

• Another strategy that several people reported was to invite one or more of their executives to accompany them to national conferences—particularly when the conferences were held in exotic locations. They attended sessions together and discussed their applications to "back-home" situations. In fact, I have been impressed with the number of my colleagues in the ASTD I have met at ASTD conferences who introduced their companions to me as "my boss."

• Many HRD professionals have used the strategy of volunteering to make presentations or (preferably) to put on demonstrations at staff meetings, executive retreats, and other gatherings of executives. Several of my former students have told me that this strategy backfires if it is too slick, propagandistic, or self-serving. It works best when executives are provided with an authentic experience with andragogical learning designs dealing with concerns that are real to them and are treated as active participants with a chance to give evaluative feedback.

• The management development group at Westinghouse Electric Corporation tells me that one of the most valuable payoffs of its Executive Forum program has been the involvement of key executives of the corporation as resource people in various sessions. For several years they have made a point of drawing the top people from various corporate divisions, subsidiaries, and plants, almost on a rotating schedule, to serve as learning resources for the management trainees. Sometimes they are asked to make presentations, but often they are invited to submit to a sort of "Meet the Press" interview by a panel of participants as to what it is really like to climb up the corporate ladder and where they found the "weak rungs" to be. Staff members tell me that this hands-on experience with management development has resulted in dramatically increased understanding of and support for the HRD program.

• Another strategy that several people reported is to bring in an outsider as a resource person to the executive group—a professor of adult education, a well-known consultant, a member of the leadership group of the ASTD or AMA, or, perhaps best of all, an executive from another corporation who has had a successful experience with a program based on principles of adult learning. One of the best experiences I have had with this strategy occurred when the director of HRD of the Lloyds Bank of California invited me to come to Los Angeles several years ago to meet with the HRD staff for a day (in which they coached me more than I them) and then to meet with the top corporate executives the next day in a seminar on "Modern Principles and Strategies of Adult Learning." I found the executives to be open, eager, and responsive learners. And the HRD director told me that support for the HRD program increased visibly following this session.

Q. How do you get people to be self-directed learners?
A. I start with a big "don't." You don't just throw people into the strange waters of self-directed learning and hope that they can swim. This is a new experience for many people, and they need some preparation for it. Always before, they have been told by someone else—a teacher or trainer— what they are going to learn, how they are going to learn it, when they are going to learn it, and whether they have learned it. The notion that they are going to have to take some responsibility for making these decisions for themselves typically induces a high level of anxiety. A little anxiety, I explain, stimulates learning; but each of us has an anxiety ceiling that if exceeded operates as a block to learning. So I always open a self-directed learning activity with an orienta- tion session.

My orientation sessions vary from an hour or so for a one-day workshop to three or four hours for a one-semester course to a full day or more for a long-term supervisory- or management-development program. The same components are present in all three designs, the difference in time being accounted for by the depth to which they go in each compo- nent. The components of the design are as follows:

1.   A relationship-building, climate-setting exercise. I introduce this exercise by explaining that learning is facili- tated by a climate in which participants see themselves as mutual helpers rather than as competitors, in which there is mutual trust—among learners and between learners and the trainer—in which people feel safe and supportive rather than threatened and judgmental, and in which everyone feels re- spected. I ask the participants to form small groups of four or five each and share these things about themselves in each group:

- *What* they are (in Martin Buber's terms, their "It-It" rela- tionship): their present work roles and previous experience

- *Who* they are (Buber's "I-Thou" relationship): namely, one thing about themselves that will enable others to see them as unique human beings, different from everyone else in the room
- Any special resources they have that are relevant to this program, gained through previous experience or study, that would be useful for others to know about
- Any questions, problems, or concerns that they are hoping will be dealt with in this program

I role model what I am hoping this exercise will produce by giving this information about myself. When I sense that the groups have completed this task, I invite one or two members of each group to summarize what they learned about the other members of the group.

2. A cognitive map of self-directed learning. This is a short presentation summarizing the main findings of recent research about the characteristics of adults as learners, namely that (a) they have a deep psychological need to be self-directing, (b) they bring into any learning situation resources from their previous experience and training that are a rich resource for one another's learning, (c) they are task centered, problem centered, and life centered in their orientation to learning, and (d) they are intrinsically motivated to learn given the right conditions and encouragement. I emphasize that what people learn through their own initiative they usually learn more effectively and retain longer than what is didactically transmitted to them by others.

3. Skill-practice exercises. After explaining that a different set of skills is required for self-directed learning from those required in learning from a teacher, I engage the participants in one or more exercises designed to develop such skills as diagnosing their own needs for learning, reading a book proactively rather than reactively, interviewing resource people, and giving and receiving help.

4. Construction of a learning contract. I have them read a handout I have prepared, "Some Guidelines for Using Learning Contracts" (Knowles, 1975, p. 129), that describes

step-by-step how to go about drafting a learning contract. Then I invite each participant to draft a minicontract for some simple objective, such as "improving my ability to make a speech," and then share their contracts in groups of three or four.

5. The final component is an invitation to the participants to raise any unresolved questions or issues about self-directed learning, to which I respond.

One final note: I have found that as a group of people are launched into a self-directed learning process it greatly enhances the chances of long-run payoffs if they are organized into informal "learning networks" of from three to six people to give one another continuing support.

Q. Do people really want to be self-directing?

A. The fact is that adults are self-directing when they undertake to learn something on their own. In his extensive investigation of adult learning, Allen Tough (1979) has found that self-directed learning is a normal and universal activity among adults. But he has also found that often adults do not consider what they have learned outside of an educational institution as being "education." When he asked his subjects, "Have you learned anything in the past year?" a frequent response was, "No, I haven't attended any classes." However, when he probed into whether they were doing anything different this year, they were able to describe an average of eight major learning projects in which they took the initiative to find resources—material and human—from which they learned something.

There is growing evidence that adults do want to be self-directing, in fact that they have a deep psychological need to be self-directing (Cross, 1976; Gross, 1977; Houle, 1961; Kidd, 1973; Knox, 1977; Loevinger, 1976; Maslow, 1970; Rogers, 1969; Penland, 1977; Tough, 1967). We become adult psychologically when we come to perceive ourselves as being essentially responsible for our own lives. And, as I have said before, at that point we develop a deep psychological need for others to perceive us and to treat us as being capable of taking responsibility for ourselves. This creates a problem for us in adult education in general and training in particular. Adults come to us with years of conditioning in their previous school experience to perceive the role of "student" as being a dependent role. In fact, they put a lot of pressure on us to treat them as children because that is their preconception as to what education is. If we give in to this pressure and start treating them as dependent learners, we put them into a psychological conflict between this intellectualized conception of the role of learner and their deeper psychological need to be self-directing.

And how do people deal with psychological conflict? Typically, by trying to flee from it—which in education we call "resistance to learning" or "poor motivation" or "dropping out." Hence, the importance of providing adult learners with the kind of orientation experience described in the preceding section.

Q. Is everybody capable of being a self-directed learner?
A. I suppose there are some people who are pathologically dependent, but if so, they are more likely to be found in mental institutions than in the normal community. I must confess that I have been almost at the point of giving up a few times, but I have yet to meet anybody who hasn't been able to take at least some responsibility for his or her own learning unless he or she is entering into a body of content that is totally strange. My assumption is that if we fail to engage people in taking some responsibility, it is more likely to be our fault than theirs. We still have much to learn about how to help people acquire the concepts, attitudes, and skills required to be self-directed learners.

Q. Is self-directed learning the best form of education in all situations?
A. I am sure it isn't even appropriate, much less best, in all situations. If I had been a passenger on the *Titanic*, I would not have wanted the captain to have me construct a

learning contract specifying how I would learn what to do in case we hit an iceberg. I believe that straight indoctrination is an appropriate form of education in some situations, particularly where protection of human life is involved. And I believe that in other situations direct didactic instruction is appropriate, such as how to operate a machine the learner has never seen before. Nevertheless, whenever more complex human performances are involved, especially those requiring judgment, insight, creativity, planning, problem solving, self-confidence, and the like, I think that self-directed learning is appropriate.

Q.   Are all instructors capable of learning to be facilitators of self-directed learning?
A.   It has been my experience that they are. The secret to launching them in this direction, I think, is to have them experience being treated as adult learners and then analyzing how they feel about it and how it happened. In my one-day workshops we spend most of the morning setting an adult learning climate, having participants diagnose their own needs and interests and formulate their learning objectives, and planning learning experiences to accomplish those objectives. In the afternoon we explore the assumptions about learning in the pedagogical and andragogical models and then identify the strategies employed in applying the andragogical model and the role of the facilitator in the entire process. But I am impressed by how many reports I have received from teachers and trainers describing how they have made the transition from teacher to facilitator simply by reading about it (Cross, 1976; Kidd, 1973; Knowles, 1975, 1980, 1984; Knowles and Associates, 1984) and then experimenting with facilitating self-directed learning. Many people report that they experienced acquiring a different set of psychic rewards. Instead of getting their kicks out of controlling learners, they experienced the joy that comes from releasing learners—from seeing the energy that is released when learners get excited about learning, from working on their own self-planned learning projects.

Q. Are learning contracts an essential ingredient of self-directed learning?

A. No, but they are the most effective devices I have yet discovered for helping learners organize their learning in a systematic, individualized, self-paced, process-structured way. Learning contracts are being used extensively now in educational institutions, business and industry, government agencies, and voluntary organizations (Knowles and Associates, 1984; Knowles, 1986).

Q. How does one deal with time constraints in learning? For example, we are often asked to cover several hours' worth of content in one hour.

A. My first reaction to this question is that I think that as professionals we have an obligation to stand up and object when unrealistic time limits are imposed on us. We need to be able to provide our policymakers with realistic estimates of the time that will be required to accomplish particular objectives and to give clear and convincing reasons why this is so.

A second reaction is that the assumption that all content must be "covered" in a meeting—that the only learning that occurs takes place in a classroom or workshop—places an unfair burden on a teacher or trainer and denigrates the role and dignity of the learners. The important thing is not that the content be "covered" but that it be acquired by the learners. And there are many ways they can acquire content, including through independent study, peer-helping groups, interviews with resource people, field projects, multimedia packages, and computer-assisted instruction. Here is where I find learning contracts to be an especially useful device for helping learners to plan how they are going to acquire required content by making use of a variety of resources and strategies.

Q. How can adult educators and trainers bring about institutional change?

A. As I see it, three strategies are used to bring about

institutional change. One is "change by edict." But this strategy is available to us only if we are in a position to issue edicts and enforce them, which eliminates most of us practitioners. A second strategy is "change by persuasion." This strategy is effective only if we are in positions from which people will listen to us and if we are persuasive, which eliminates many of the rest of us. But a third strategy is available to all of us, and in the long run it probably produces more stable, lasting, and constructive change than the other strategies: "change by piloting or demonstration and osmosis."

For example, when I started the graduate program in adult education at Boston University in 1960, I was committed to making it as congruent with principles of adult learning as I could. I knew that this would mean violating some of the sacred cows of academia, such as normal-curve grading, prescribed common objectives, standardized testing, assigned reading, brilliant lectures, and the like. So I knew I would not be able to get prior approval from the graduate committee. And I questioned the wisdom of even trying to persuade my faculty colleagues to support me; they would feel threatened by some radical upstart. So I chose the third strategy and started experimenting in my own classroom and with my own students in applying such andragogical concepts as self-diagnosis of learning needs, peer inquiry teams, learning contracts, mutual negotiation of grades, and the like. Within a couple of years my students had become so enthusiastic about being given shared responsibility for the learning process that they began asking other professors to let them do learning contracts with them, and some of the professors were intrigued and went along. As they started experiencing success in getting students excited about learning, the professors began to adopt some of the strategies. Thus, osmosis took place through the influence of the students. I later learned that the osmosis process could be speeded up if I invited two or three faculty members to observe what I was doing and give me evaluative reactions. They got "hooked" by observing the results but, most important, did not feel that I was trying to change them.

Q. What do you think of the liberationist educators such as Paulo Freire and Ivan Illich?

A. I find it difficult to think of Freire and Illich in the same category. I see Freire (1970) as being a highly innovative, socially concerned, activist adult educator. I have gained a good deal of inspiration and many methodological suggestions from his writings. I find Illich (1970) to be essentially a nihilist, and although he has caused me to reexamine my assumptions, social philosophy, and value system occasionally, I can't think of much constructive help I have gleaned from his writings. My general reaction is that Illich is against the existing system, period, whereas Freire is for changing it. And I am, too.

In principle, I support challenges to the way things are, even nihilistic challenges. I think our educational enterprise is energized by them.

Q. What do you think of mandatory continuing professional education?

A. Ideally, I favor all adult education's being voluntary. It is my experience that voluntary learners are usually more committed learners than those who are participating under compulsion. But I can empathize with society's wanting the security of knowing that its professionals, particularly in the health professions, are keeping up to date. My hope, if not conviction, is that mandatory continuing professional education is a transitional phenomenon. I believe that when the concept of continuing professional development becomes imbedded in the heart of what it means to be a professional, mandatory professional continuing education will fade away. But this process will be greatly facilitated if the notion of continuing professional education becomes a part of the core curriculum of preprofessional education. Our schools of medicine, nursing, law, and so on will, I feel certain, incorporate principles and strategies of self-directed learning in their undergraduate curricula—as many of them are doing already.

Q. Does adult education maintain, increase, or reduce the social and economic inequalities in American society?

A. As things stand to date, I think that adult education increases inequalities, because studies of participation (Cross, 1981; Knox, 1977) show that the more education people have, the more likely they are to participate in adult educational activities. This is an intolerable situation. We cannot afford to enter the twenty-first century with one-fifth of our population functionally illiterate; therefore, it must become a high-priority national policy to mount a crash program to deliver adult educational services to our undereducated fellow citizens at their convenience in terms of time, place, and pace, as well as in terms of their needs to perform life roles effectively. Courses in reading, writing, and arithmetic are not the answer. Adult Performance Level programs are what are needed. And since this is a national problem, federal financing is required.

Q. What do you see the role of professional associations to be in serving the cause and the discipline of adult education?

A. I see the primary role of membership associations (AAACE and ASTD, especially) at this stage of the development of our field as being to provide opportunities for continuing professional development. Their publications, conferences, and other activities should be seen as being primarily resources for the professional development of their members. A secondary role is to provide a vehicle for professional identification and fellowship. Adult education is in a fairly early stage of development as a field of professional study and practice, so it is still in the process of defining itself. Adult educators, therefore, need help in defining what their role is in society and in working together in this quest. Finally, I think there is a need for the adult education movement to be interpreted to the public and to have advocates in influencing public policy toward greater support for the goal of increasing lifelong learning opportunities for all our citizens. Membership organizations have typically performed this function in our democracy. A more specialized need is for a systematic development of the body of theory and practice of the adult educational discipline. This is the role that the Commission of Professors of Adult Education has been trying to perform—in my estimation, quite effectively.

Q.   What do you see as your major contributions to the field of adult education, and how do you evaluate them?

A.   The contribution that has without doubt made the greatest impact in terms of theory, practice, and research is my andragogical model. I accept and feel deep satisfaction from other people's evaluations such as these:

• Tennant (1986): "Many commentators have noted the popular appeal of Knowles' theory of andragogy and have highlighted its shortcomings. Nevertheless, its popularity remains undiminished, as evidenced by Knowles and Associates' most recent publication, *Andragogy in Action,* which documents the application of his ideas across a broad spectrum of institutions" (p. 113).

• Cross (1981): "Whether andragogy can serve as the foundation for a unifying theory of adult education remains to be seen. At the very least, it identifies some characteristics of adult learners that deserve attention. It has been far more successful than most theory in gaining the attention of practitioners, and it has been moderately successful in sparking debate; it has not been especially successful, however, in stimulating research to test the assumptions" (pp. 227–228). (Regarding this last point, the situation has changed considerably since 1981; an increasing volume of research has tended to support the assumptions.)

• Boyer (1984): "The intent of Malcolm Knowles and Carl Rogers in introducing their theories to modern educators was to contribute to the actualization of the learner faced with outmoded institutions of schooling. They further realized the potential unity among humanistic educators of adults and children. Perhaps, with flexibility, variety, deeper understanding, and broadened skills offered by the two theories, a new consolidation of effort may be the outcome. It is conceivable that Knowles and Rogers would welcome a further realization of their vision in this manner" (p. 20).

. • Gross (1982): "The single most influential concept in contemporary American adult education is Malcolm Knowles's 'andragogy.' . . . Here are just some of the pervasive practices in present-day adult education that owe much of their acceptance to Knowles's powerful concept:

*treating students and clients like dignified, competent human beings

*providing a climate and environment more congenial to adults than a schoolroom atmosphere

*basing offerings on the expressed needs of students

*organizing presentations and courses to involve students actively in their own learning

*having students learn about one another's strengths and resources so they can use one another as learning resources" (p. 144).

I think that I have contributed to the broadening and deepening of our understanding of the nature of the adult educational movement in this country and its historical roots. I am pleased with how often my two major books on this subject, *Handbook of Adult Education in the United States* (1960) and *The Adult Education Movement in the United States* (1977), as well as several articles on the subject, are cited in other articles and books and in dissertations.

I am willing to take a little credit for the fact that the adult educational enterprise in this country is an open system. While I was executive director of the Adult Education Association of the U.S.A. from 1951 to 1959, there was an energetic movement to institute a process of certification and to limit membership in the association to certified professionals. I, along with the majority of our delegate assembly, resisted this pressure on the score that much of the richness and vitality of the field of adult education could be attributed to its attracting people from a variety of backgrounds and disciplines.

I have contributed somewhat to the literature of self-directed learning, program planning, and a theoretical base for research in our field. My role in these contributions has been more that of a practitioner than a scholar—a role with which I feel more comfortable.

Finally, I perceive that my most satisfying contribution
has been in facilitating the development of several hundred
students who worked with me on their degrees in adult education at Boston University, North Carolina State University,
Nova University, the Union Graduate School, and the Fielding Institute. Those former students are making the andragogical model work and are pushing forward the frontiers of
research in our field.

In retrospect, I can see that I could have made other
contributions if I had devoted time and energy to them.
I could have given more assertive leadership to creating
mechanisms for involving our field in public policy-making,
particularly when I was the executive director of the Adult
Education Association of the U.S.A. I could have established
a better balance between action research (which is mostly
what I did) and experimental research. I could have done a
better job of establishing stronger links with adult educators
in other countries. On the whole, though, I have no regrets
about putting my emphases where I did.

Chapter 6

How I Am Evaluated and How I React to and Use Evaluations

The term *evaluation* is used with several meanings in education. Perhaps the most common meaning is the quality and effectiveness of a total program—a workshop, course, conference, or curriculum. A second meaning is the measurement of the amount and quality of learning the learners accomplished. A third meaning, which is drawing increasing and controversial attention in formal educational institutions, is the quality and effectiveness of teachers. Because there is a strong flavor of judgment (good, mediocre, poor) in the concept of evaluation, those being evaluated have approached it with a good deal of apprehension and, often, resistance.

For thirty years I have subscribed to the definition propounded by Kempfer (1955, p. 399): "The basic purpose of evaluation is to stimulate growth and improvement. Whatever other worthy purposes exist are only facets of the all-inclusive effort to assess present conditions as a basis for achieving better ones. Evaluation that does not lead to improved practice is sterile."

In this chapter, therefore, I shall describe the ways I have attempted to get information that will help me to improve my practice from three sources: (1) the participants in workshops and courses, (2) correspondence with individuals, and (3) critiques appearing in the literature. The data

101

from these sources include all three meanings cited in the first paragraph.

Evaluations in Workshops and Courses

As I explain in the section "Learning About Meaning-ful Evaluation" in Chapter Two, I ask small groups of the participants in my workshops and courses to generate evaluative statements about the quality of the experience and what learning they got from it that they intend to implement in their jobs or their lives.

End-of-Meeting Evaluations

Here is an example of the recorders' reports from one workshop, "Understanding and Working with Adult Learners," with the training managers of the U.S. Department of Health and Human Services in 1986 (A = agree, D = disagree):

Group 1 (N = 5)

I got something I could take back and apply immediately to my work. (A = 5, D = 0)

Helpful in reinforcing previous learnings. (A = 3, D = 0)

References to other publications were helpful so I could continue my self-development. (A = 5, D = 0)

Helpful to discuss with others how I would apply what I learned. (A = 5, D = 0)

Model for what he teaches and good pacing (changes, breaks, etc.) were helpful. (A = 5, D = 0)

Self-diagnostic rating scale was good in concept and format; appreciate his saying we could use it (no copyright issue). (A = 5, D = 0)

Group 2 (N = 8)

What about the format of the workshop was useful? Multiple breaks, relaxed learning atmosphere. (A = 8, D = 0)

What was effective about the instructor? Depth of knowledge, willingness to share (including non-copyright materials), ability to model his principles, personal anecdotal experiences, which made it real and noncondescending. ($A = 8, D = 0$)

What did we get out of session? Ideas that we feel are practical, balance of methods for facilitating learning—lecture and group work, not one or the other. ($A = 8, D = 0$)

Group 3 (N = 5)

I liked the exercises—most useful reinforcement and nice diversion. ($A = 5, D = 0$)

Length too long; half a day would have had more impact. ($A = 5, D = 0$)

Very diverse group made it difficult to structure workshop—and made it more real. ($A = 5, D = 0$)

Excellent reinforcement of andragogical philosophy. ($A = 5, D = 0$)

Group 4 (N = 4)

Opened and enlarged my thinking about adult learning concepts. ($A = 4, D = 0$)

Good participatory climate in both small groups and larger group. ($A = 4, D = 0$)

I'm going to take back learning contract—good practical knowledge, practical applications. ($A = 4, D = 0$)

Malcolm was frank, forthcoming; gave good answers. ($A = 4, D = 0$)

The references, bibliography were useful. ($A = 4, D = 0$)

Malcolm makes you feel comfortable in terms of relating to other workshop participants. ($A = 4, D = 0$)

I appreciated Malcolm's sensitivity to the fact that we've been sitting here all day—frequent breaks, exercises. ($A = 4, D = 0$)

Malcolm's presentations were very interesting and laced with levity; no tuning out. ($A = 4, D = 0$)

Concept of transfer of learning was very useful, very
practical. (A = 4, D = 0)

Mostly Positive Evaluations. These comments are
quite typical of the evaluations I have been receiving in
recent years. Almost all of them mention their positive feelings about the relaxed, respectful, participatory, informal
climate—which also makes me a bit sad that this should be
such a noteworthy phenomenon. I frequently get the comment, "This workshop was fun," which I think all learning
experiences should be. I am also pleased with how often I
get a comment about how the workshop reinforced previous
learnings, ideas, or intuitions. I believe that all learning experiences should be reinforcing as well as stretching. I also get
frequent comments about the pace or tempo of the workshop.
I have a rule of thumb that no activity should last more than
thirty or forty minutes without a change to another activity
or a break, and this practice is almost universally approved
(although I occasionally get the comment, "too many
breaks"). I seldom get the comment that the workshop was
too long; more often the complaint is that it was too short,
that it should have been two days instead of one. For example, in a workshop I did with the Missouri Cooperative
Extension Service in 1981, one participant commented,
"Shorter time span; follow printed agenda; too long." In the
same list of comments were these: "Knowles is one of the few
HRD practitioners who has more than one day's worth of
interesting information, make it longer: two or three days";
"2 days or longer"; "2 days, not one, but this was great."

*Not All Evaluations Are Positive, and Some Are Con-
tradictory.* Not all evaluations have been positive, of course,
particularly those of workshops I did in earlier years. For
example, in a workshop I did with the Dallas ASTD in 1980,
I got the comment, "Too much time spent in anecdotes; example, over 5 minutes with statistics story—funny but of little
value." I make a point of illustrating principles with descriptions of personal experiences (which in the current literature

would be referred to as the use of imagery). This comment caused me to become aware of the fact that I sometimes get carried away with my stories and give more detail than is warranted. I can testify that my "anecdotes" have become much shorter as a result of the helpful feedback I got in Dallas.

I often get contradictory comments. In the same Dallas ASTD workshop, for example, one participant said, "Did not seem to practice what you preach," while another participant said, "Malcolm Knowles *practices* what he preaches. It is so refreshing and made the seminar effective for me." In a Missouri Cooperative Extension Service workshop one participant said, "Less info on contract learning—too much time spent on this," while another said, "In afternoon session, more work on contracts." In a workshop with the human resources development staff of the Steelcase Corporation in 1985 two participants agreed with the statement "We would like to see additional media used in the presentations (i.e., movies, video, slides)" and three disagreed. In a number of workshops some participants commented that too much time was spent in small group work while many others cited this aspect of the workshop as most valuable.

The way I process these contradictions is to accept the fact that there is always a wide range of differences in a group of adults—differences in background, experience, interests, motivation, speed of learning, learning styles, and abilities. I try everything I can to individualize the learning strategies so as to provide for individual differences, but I accept the reality that I can't satisfy everybody equally. My rationalization is that if not more than 10 percent of the participants are relatively dissatisfied, I have at least bettered the curve of normal distribution.

Evaluation Through Back-Home Application

Another form of evaluation I sometimes use is to ask the participants to identify what they have learned at the workshop that they plan to use "back home." Perhaps the most frequent response is exemplified by this statement from a participant in a workshop with the Aramco Services Company in Houston in 1984: "I will create a climate that is more conducive to learning in a statistics class I am teaching." (Many people have told me that the idea of creating an atmosphere that is conducive to learning is the first element in the andragogical model that they apply in their practice.) Other statements from the same workshop include: "I will use the information in establishing a climate and managing change *immediately* in planning for an organizational merger." "I will develop competency-based criteria for appraising current training staff performance." "I will share this workshop with young adult sons who are in the corporate world." "I will use the qualitative evaluation procedures in the Religious Education Commission in my church." "I plan to design instructional materials taking into account adult learners' needs for self-direction."

Other comments about application plans from a workshop with the Eastern Maine Healthcare Human Resources Development program in 1984 include: "Plan and practice for the transfer of training." "At least explore the possibilities of implementing learning contracts in a technical- and skill-oriented program." "Develop a competency model for training programs." "I plan to develop an orientation program that is competency based and involves learning contracts."

From a workshop sponsored by the University of Surrey, England, in 1986: "Intend to use case examples to give encouragement that the ideals of self-directed learning can become a reality." "Confidence to develop contract learning within our own fields, but have not resolved the difficulties of coping with time and institutional constraints." "Helen will reorganize briefing days to include different orientation methods." "Yvonne will follow up contacts made here to develop ideas." "Develop competency model specifically for group work course." "More reading in the area of andragogy." "Will use contract/competency-based education with junior midwifery students." "Will use the self-diagnostic rating scale with teachers coming to the end of their year's training." "Will report on this day to peer colleagues." "Make a learning contract with myself."

In the last analysis, I find that the reporting of plans for back-home application is the most telling form of evaluation. I close my workshops with a "benediction" in which I share with the participants what my aspirations for the day were as I began. It goes like this: "My first aspiration was that you would experience being treated as adult learners during the day and would leave here with a deep commitment to treat your students and clients as adult learners. My second aspiration was that you would find that you received reinforcement for many things you have intuitively been thinking or doing. My third aspiration was that you would pick up some new ideas or adaptations of old ideas that make sense to you and that you would like to experiment with in your practice. My fourth aspiration was that you would leave here with a little bit more courage than you came with to try out principles and techniques you have experienced here. My fifth aspiration was that you would have identified some people here with interests similar to yours with whom you can network. My sixth aspiration was that you would leave here with some plans (such as learning contracts) for continuing your own personal and professional development when you get back home. My final aspiration was that you would have found today to be a pleasurable experience; that you would have had fun. And I can testify that you have made it fun for me."

The evaluations I receive give me assurance that most of these aspirations have been realized as regards most participants.

Evaluations Led to Two New Books

Finally, workshop evaluations have resulted in two books. In the late 1970s and early 1980s I received a number of comments to the effect that "We would like to know how the andragogical model is being applied in institutions like ours." As a result I began inviting workshop participants to send me descriptive reports of how they were using the andra-gogical model in their institutions. By 1983 I had received more than thirty reports, and I brought them together (with commentary by me) in a book, *Andragogy in Action,* published by Jossey-Bass in 1984. I had also been getting comments to the effect that participants would like to see examples of actual learning contracts developed in a variety of insti-tutions. Through a similar process I obtained descriptions of how contract learning was being used, with examples of actual contracts, in twenty-six institutions and presented them in a book, *Using Learning Contracts,* published in 1986 by Jossey-Bass.

Correspondence with Individuals

One of the richest sources of psychic reward in my life is letters I receive from former students, participants in work-shops, and even people who have merely read my books or articles. I typically receive several such letters each month; our mail carrier knows me well. I will share excerpts from a small sample of letters I have received during the last three years.

The first letter is from a former student at Boston Uni-versity who has had her own consulting firm in California for several years and describes a most unexpected application of my principles: "Malcolm, I have written you so many let-ters in my head over the years! I wonder if you have any idea of the ways in which you and andragogy and its values have become the core of me? We had, four years ago this week, an andragogical wedding process; a wonderful, open, sharing and spontaneous affair in my little hillside house on New Year's morning. Just an hour ago George's 25-year-old son came by with his fiancée and said they wanted a wedding like ours next fall."

This letter comes from a faculty member at Florida State University: "As a visiting professor teaching Adult Edu-cation in Home Economics at the Brigham Young University for the Summer Term, I have just today finished reading your excellent book *The Modern Practice of Adult Education.* It has given me new insights into my role as a teacher, and I am excited about the prospects of applying your many fine ideas in my classes. . . . Thank you for the format of your text, which makes it practical. Never before have I read a book cover-to-cover, marking on every page and referring to every example in the Appendix and Exhibits. They are all most interesting and helpful."

The next letter is from a faculty member at the University of California, Davis: "This is to express my appreciation once again for your taking the time to join the staff of University Extension. . . . Without exception, the academic staff who attended the meeting told me that the morning was exhilarating for them. . . . I think that the personal experiences that you related and your thoughts on adult and continuing education validated the career choices many of us have made. . . . On a personal note, some of us were fascinated with the skills that you have as a group leader. Your few hours with us have set a model for accomplishment for those of us who came out of other fields and have inadvertently made careers in adult education."

Here is a report from a training officer in a southern bank: "I thoroughly enjoyed your ASTD workshop yesterday. Your warmth, enthusiasm, sense of humor, and high regard for others set you apart from the 'experts' who 'perform.' I left the workshop feeling renewed, reaffirmed, and sorry I couldn't stay for the evening meeting."

Next is an excerpt from an interview in the *Bay Area O.D. Journal* with a San Francisco training consultant on heroes in her life: "For someone to be a hero, it is not enough that s/he have ideas (new or reinterpreted). I look for a congruence that says a person practices what s/he preaches. I had the good fortune of participating in a seminar that Malcolm Knowles ran and experienced that congruence and a person who is willing to share and help others grow. I consider him a special person and a hero."

Finally (this delicious massage has to end some time), this statement was passed along to me from a most surprising source—my son, Dr. Eric S. Knowles, a professor of psychology at the University of Arkansas. A woman whom he had interviewed for admission to the doctoral program in his department wrote him: "What I couldn't quite muster the articulate speech to say was that your father's work led me to the most rewarding experience of my life, that of teaching English to adult immigrants and to returning veterans, as well as 'mainstream' adults. His enthusiasm, encouragement, and common sense coupled with sound educational theory led me to understand the nature of what I was doing and hopefully helped me to do it better. Working toward this doctorate means everything to me, and if I succeed, part of the credit belongs to your dad. You also showed me that his son is warm, charming, and altogether delightful." (I hope she was accepted.)

Evaluations Reflect a Process More Than a Personality

If my statements in this chapter seem to be coming from a "stacked deck" of only positive feedback, they are not. I chose them more or less at random, with the only criterion for selection being the assurance of some distribution among types of institutional and geographical settings, from forty-nine unsolicited letters I had received from 1983 to 1986. Probably some sort of self-selection process was at work: people with less positive feelings are less likely to write letters, I suppose. While these kinds of positive reactions make me feel good personally, I interpret them less as reactions to me as a person (although some of the statements are put in these terms) and more as reflections of the potency of the andragogical process, which I happened to be managing. Many of my former students, a number of them with personalities quite different from mine, report that they receive the same kind of reactions. What I perceive is being evaluated, therefore, is the process rather than me as a person. What is so reassuring to me is that this is a process that almost anyone with a commitment to helping people learn can learn to manage; it is not dependent on "gift" or "personality."

Critiques Appearing in the Literature

Since 1970, when I first presented my andragogical model in book form in *The Modern Practice of Adult Education,* a number of articles and books have appeared supporting the model and often describing case examples of how it was applied in a variety of situations with superior results. In a growing number of research studies—many of them dissertations—various aspects of the model have been subjected to empirical testing and on the whole have been supported. This is the kind of positive evaluation my work has received, and I react with gratitude.

Another series of articles and books that began appearing in 1973 have taken a more critical stance toward the model. This body of literature has frequently been referred to as "the andragogical debate." The most recent example I know of is an article by Ronald L. Podeschi, "Andragogy: Proofs or Premises" (1987), which presents an overview of the "debate" and concludes that "Even to raise the issue of so-called 'neutral' research, and to urge critical attention to assumptions underlying research in adult education, is to take a philosophical stance. A primary premise of this author is that debate about research, like debate about andragogy, involves philosophical as well as empirical issues. Since philosophical questions are answered ultimately by beliefs and purposes, practitioners should be wary of covert epistemology and values underlying adult education research—whether about andragogy or any other topic" (p. 16).

My own philosophical orientation has its roots in the humanistic, pragmatic, and existential frameworks of John Dewey, Eduard Lindeman, Abraham Maslow, Carl Rogers, and their associates, as I spell out in *The Adult Learner: A Neglected Species* (1984, pp. 85–105). I believe in the fundamental goodness of human beings, in their right to self-determination, in their almost infinite potential, in their latent ability to self-actualize, and in their innate ability to learn. I believe with Dewey in the central role of experience in learning and with Lindeman in the intrinsic relationship between learning and living. I also believe that environmental conditions can—and often do—inhibit the fulfillment of these beliefs and that part of the mission of adult educators is to influence environment. I also believe that the philosophical premises of the behaviorists, such as Skinner, and the cognitive theorists, such as Bruner and Gagne, are in touch with some of the realities of the human condition, and I have no hesitation about applying them when they are relevant to a given situation. (For example, I make a good deal of use of Skinner's concept of reinforcement and Bruner's concept of intelligence-driven discovery.) So I accept (and glory in) the criticism that I am a philosophical eclectic or situationalist who applies his philosophical beliefs differentially to different situations. I see myself as being free from any single ideological dogma, and so I don't fit neatly into any of the categories philosophers often want to box people into.

A criticism that has been leveled against andragogy several times is that it is not a theory. My problem with this is that in the social science literature there appears to be little agreement as to the meaning of the word *theory*. *Webster's Ninth New Collegiate Dictionary* gives two definitions that apply to this kind of situation: (1) "The analysis of a set of facts in their relation to one another" and (2) "A belief, policy, or procedure proposed or followed as the basis of action." I believe that andragogy qualifies as a theory according to both definitions. However, I prefer to think of it as a model of assumptions about learning or a conceptual framework that serves as a basis for an emergent theory. It certainly has served its purpose as a stimulant for a growing body of theoretical thinking in our field, and I thoroughly applaud this use of it.

How Criticism Helped Me Change

Another criticism that was made especially in the 1970s was that the andragogical model dichotomized assumptions about learning in children and learning in adults. It is true that in my original presentation of the andragogical model, in *The Modern Practice of Adult Education* in 1970, I did make such a dichotomy. As a result of this criticism and new research regarding learning in children, in the 1980 revised edition of the book I changed the dichotomy to a continuum, proposing that when pedagogical assumptions are realistic (as when the learner is truly dependent on receiving instruction upon entering a totally strange new territory of subject matter), pedagogical strategies are appropriate—but only up to the point at which the learner has acquired sufficient knowledge of the content to be able to start engaging in self-directed inquiry about it. My perception now is that recent experiments in elementary and secondary schools have revealed that children and youth are able to take much more responsibility for their own learning than the traditional pedagogical model predicted. As a result, the andragogical theory has become a general theory about learning, subsuming the pedagogical assumptions but placing them in the initial stages of totally new learning.

Some Criticism of Criticisms

A fairly frequent criticism is that the andragogical theory has not been tested empirically. I have several reactions to this criticism. The first is that while there was very little research on the theory in the first few years, a growing volume of research, both quantitative and qualitative, has been reported in the literature from around the world in the last decade. The qualitative and action-research studies have tended to support and refine the theory.

My second reaction is that much of the quantitative research tends to focus on one element of the theory and ignore its interdependence with other elements. For example, several studies have used quantitative instruments to test the proposition that adults are self-directed in their learning, particularly in formal educational settings, and have found that they are not. A point I have made repeatedly in my writings is that when adults enter into an academic setting, they hark back to their earlier conditioning in schooling to be dependent learners. In order for them to be comfortable with and able to engage in self-directed learning, they need to have a reorientation experience through which they come to perceive learning as an active process of inquiry and to acquire the skills to engage in self-directed inquiry. Several ways to help them become skillful self-directed learners are spelled out in my books *Self-Directed Learning: A Guide for Learners and Teachers* (Knowles, 1975) and *Andragogy in Action* (Knowles and Associates, 1984).

A third reaction is that when critics use the term *empirical* they often limit it to controlled laboratory experiments or statistical correlational research. My own observation is that when the phenomena being investigated are about learning and human growth and development, such qualitative methods as case studies, diaries, and action research have been much more productive than quantitative methods. And these fit the definition of *empirical,* too.

Others have occasionally criticized my advocacy of the use of learning contracts as a way to help learners plan and organize their learning. Many critics interpret my position as being a rigid imposition of a universal panacea that boxes learners into a narrow inquiry that interferes with exploratory or divergent learning. They misread my intentions. I repeatedly point out that contract learning is not a panacea appropriate for all occasions but a tool to assist learners when they are fairly clear about what they want to learn. I also maintain that learning contracts should be treated as infinitely renegotiable as learners discover new objectives and resources in the process of carrying out their contracts. I have a hunch that the very term *contract* implies a rigidity that is associated with its legal use. I suggest that in situations in which this presents a problem the term *learning plan* or *learning agreement* be used instead. In the literature *learning contract* is used most frequently. These same critics also sometimes suggest that a learning contract opens up the possibility of a teacher's imposing his or her will on the learner, which is why I emphasize that the contracting process be treated as a process of mutually trusting and helpful negotiation between a learner and a resource person; and this implies the importance of specialized training for the resource person.

· This list by no means exhausts the critical evaluations of the andragogical theory, but I think that it represents the central thrusts of most of them. I can testify that the evaluations have been most helpful in stimulating me to engage in constant rethinking and refinement of my "theory."

Evaluation as the Stimulus for Growth

As I look back on my development as an adult educator, I can easily see that feedback regarding the consequences of my behavior has been one of the chief sources of energy for my growth. I believe that in my first few years in the profession I tended to interpret negative reactions as personal attacks or as coming from chronic complainers. But even so, I can trace many of the improvements in my professional practice during my NYA and YMCA years to reactions I received from peers and clients. It was through my experience with human relations training at the National Training Laboratories that I came to appreciate feedback as a valuable source of energy for growth, to learn how to invite it honestly, and to be able to process it nondefensively. I remember that for a while after my NTL experience I came to suspect positive feedback and almost to demand negative feedback, sometimes to the embarrassment of the feedback givers. I think that I overcame that tendency before long and came to value both kinds of feedback as valid. No doubt I became more comfortable in receiving feedback as I gained more security about my competence as a professional—an interesting paradox: evaluation (even negative) can be a way to build confidence.

Concluding Thoughts

As I reread some of the comments cited in the first two sections of this chapter, I get the feeling that they seem to be unabashedly positive and often somewhat sugary and so, apparently, self-serving. I think this is largely because I have kept evaluation reports only for the last several years. I know that reports I received during the early years (1935–1970) were more critical and contained more suggestions for improvement; therefore, they occasioned changes in my practice that caused the later reports to be more positive. As already noted, I also regard the evaluations as reflecting the andragogical process more than my personal attributes and so are more reflective of the process than the person.

Chapter 7

Technology and Education:
My Reflections and Projections

Programmed Instruction

During the 1950s I read about teaching machines, and I was curious about how such controlled instruction could involve a learner in an active process of inquiry. One of my graduate students at Boston University took a course with B. Fred Skinner in the early 1960s and reported to me that, at least at this stage in the state of the art, programmed instruction of all forms violated most of the basic principles of adult learning as I was propounding them at that time. He reported that he was bored and "turned off" by being put in the role of a reactive and penalized learner. So I was not motivated to investigate this new technology further.

A New Use of an Old Technology

My first personal experience with the use of technology for educational purposes was with the old-fashioned telephone. In the early 1960s I was asked to "teach" a twelve-week graduate course in adult learning principles to students in the School of Nursing at the University of West Virginia. The director of graduate studies there explained to me that I would have about thirty students scattered in groups of from about two to six at several locations across the state and

117

would communicate with them by telephone from my study in Newton, Massachusetts, for two hours a week. Each location would have a "speaker phone" so that students could hear me and talk with me as a group. This opportunity seemed to me to present a challenge to be creative in applying my principles of proactive, participative learning, so I accepted.

The first thing I did was to construct a "Course Learning Guide" and have it sent to the enrolled students with the request that they familiarize themselves with it and fill out the attached "Self-Diagnostic Rating Scale" before the first session. This learning guide included the following components:

- An introduction in which I described briefly who I was in terms of present position (professor of adult education at Boston University), significant past experiences, unique interests and characteristics as a person (husband of a school counselor and coauthor of two books with me, father of two "Bethelized" children, Unitarian, trout fisherman, world traveler, focal concern with the theory and practice of adult education), and my perception of my role and relationship with them as a facilitator of their learning.

- A statement of my philosophy of education and the assumptions I was making about them as adult learners and, accordingly, my perception of their role and responsibilities as students in this course.

- A description of the competency-development objectives of this course.

- A set of inquiry units identifying the questions that had to be answered to achieve the objectives of this course and the specific resources (material, experiential, and human) available to them for getting answers to these questions.

- A self-diagnostic rating scale listing the competencies this course was designed to help them develop or improve and providing a rating scale for them to use in rating the level at which each competency was important to them and the level to which they already had developed each competency through previous training or experience. Each learner, therefore, ended up with a profile showing the gaps between his or her desired level of development and his or her present level of development of each competency.

- A set of guidelines for preparing a learning plan identifying a student's learning objectives, the resources he or she planned to use in accomplishing each objective, and the evidence he or she would produce to indicate the extent to which each objective was accomplished.

At the first teleconference session I tuned in to one group after another (it turned out that there were eight groups of from three to seven students each) and asked the members of each group to introduce themselves to me (and to one another), giving the same kind of information I had given about myself in the Course Learning Guide. (Incidentally, the other groups could hear what was going on with each group.) This took about an hour. Then I asked the groups simultaneously and privately to take about fifteen minutes to identify any questions or problems they had at this point concerning the process and content described in the guide, and asked one student in each group to volunteer to give a summary of the concerns expressed. At the end of fifteen minutes I brought them back together in the teleconference and asked the volunteer reporter of each group, in turn, to report one of the concerns that seemed most pressing. I responded to each concern with some clarification and some elaboration on what was in the learning guide. This took about another half-hour, and I spent the last fifteen minutes clarifying the assignment for the next week—to prepare learning plans.

In the second session I had the students get into groups of two or three and review their learning plans with one another, identifying any questions or problems they wanted me to respond to. All groups had some questions, most of them simply seeking assurance that what they were planning was "what you want." Most of my responses were supportive, encouraging them to do what was most useful and interesting to them (within the framework of the course objectives, of course). A few questions asked for additional resources, which I was able to suggest. This activity took about an hour, and I encouraged them to take the remaining hour to begin to carry out their learning plans individually or in pairs or teams. I asked them to mail me their learning plans so I could react to them before the fourth session. (The third session was declared "research time" without a meeting.)

I had returned their learning plans to them before the fourth session, with comments about the clarity of some of their objectives, the relevance of some of their resources, and the adequacy of some of their evidence. At the beginning of that session I invited their reactions to my comments, and we did some negotiating in regard to modification of their plans. We then negotiated a time schedule for those students who wished to give oral reports during the next seven sessions. As the schedule worked out, each student had forty minutes for an oral report, with twenty minutes for my reaction and dialogue. (Incidentally, I found that I was able to inject a considerable amount of new content information—frequently information not yet available to them in printed materials—within those twenty minutes.)

The final session was devoted to evaluating the course experience and raising unresolved issues, to which I responded. The students then mailed their learning plans and portfolios of evidence to me, and I returned them within a week with my reactions and certification of the grade for which they had contracted.

I was surprised and delighted with the quality of evidence of accomplishment of their objectives they presented and, accordingly, with the quality of learning that had obviously occurred. I got a call from the director of graduate studies shortly thereafter to share with me the enthusiasm that the students had expressed to her and indicating that as a result of this success, she was planning to expand the use of courses by teleconferencing. The experience left me with a deep conviction that electronic media could indeed be used for interactive teaching and learning.

And Then Came Television

My first experience with the "sending" end of television occurred in 1952, when I was invited to host a half-hour program over a local commercial channel with a title something like "Solving Your Problems Through Learning." The sponsor was a local fur retailer who had the conviction that in order to be successful the program should be somewhat sexy; it was scheduled for midafternoon and the audience would consist mostly of housewives. I lined up some local family service agency counselors to serve as resource people to help me respond to problems phoned in by the audience. I also inveigled a couple of national adult education figures (Leland Bradford and Kenneth Benne) to serve on the panel a few times.

To be sure that we had some problems to respond to I planted a few questions with friends of mine, who used fictitious names when they called. Most of the questions had to do with learning how to deal with difficult children, husbands, relatives, and neighbors, and most of the responses from the panel consisted of referrals to community educational or counseling programs. Not many questions came from the "real" audience, and not many furs were sold. The sponsor felt that the program was not sexy enough, and it was canceled after the third week. My analysis of the experience led to the conviction that television was not a very effective instrument for involving people in learning. It also reinforced an earlier conviction that "planted" questions did not convey much emotional involvement; that, in fact, audiences sensed that they were phony.

Training for Learning by Television. Perhaps on the principle that people learn from their mistakes, I was asked to conduct "the first national training workshop for key leaders of national organizations" in Toledo, Ohio, April 20-24,

1954, under the auspices of the Council of National Organizations of the Adult Education Association of the U.S.A. I developed a working paper for this workshop titled "Learning by TV," which was reproduced in *Adult Leadership* in October 1956. In this paper I proposed five principles of adult learning and suggested the implications of each for TV programming. For example, proposition 1d: "A change is not likely to occur unless the learner chooses to have it occur, i.e., is motivated to learn. Implication for TV Programming: Find out what your audience wants to learn." Proposition 5b: "An opportunity to practice new learnings free from fear of failure will increase the likelihood that the learner will adopt the new practice. Implication for TV Programming: Stimulate the organization of 'TV Study Groups' in which viewers can practice new learnings with one another."

The Toledo workshop involved the participants in creating and enacting role-playing situations in which these principles were tested.

A Series on "The Dynamics of Leadership." An opportunity to test and further develop these principles came in 1962, when I was approached by an obviously creative and educationally curious producer, Russell Morash, for the Boston PBS station, WGBH, about collaborating with him in developing a ten-week series of half-hour programs on "The Dynamics of Leadership." The format we designed involved our inviting a variety of voluntary organizations, including the PTA, the Council of Churches, the League of Women Voters, and some thirty others, to organize local viewing groups. We supplied each participant of these viewing groups with a "Viewers' Study Guide" that suggested pre-viewing activities to prepare them to take a proactive stance toward viewing the program, activities for them to engage in while viewing the program (such as making a participation chart of the discussion group in the program), and questions for them to discuss and exercises for them to practice following the program.

Each program had a theme, such as "The Anatomy of

a Group," "Individual Motivation and Behavior in Groups," "Styles of Leadership," and the like. I gave a brief introduction in each program, managed demonstrations by a studio group (consisting of present and former students from Boston University), made periodic group process observations, and concluded with a summary of the principles being demonstrated. We also invited viewing groups to telephone or write questions, problems, and suggestions for future programs. Over two hundred viewing groups, involving almost two thousand individuals, participated, and the evaluations at the end of the series were so positive that the National Educational Television and Radio Center selected five of the programs and made them available to the entire NET network. For years since then I have met people all over the country and in Canada who have greeted me with "I saw you on television."

One-Shot Videotapes. I made videotaped single programs on "And Now We Are People" for the Group W Network in 1969, "Teaching the Adult" for the Maryland Center for Public Broadcasting in 1973, "Andragogy" for the Nebraska Educational Television Council for Higher Education in 1974, "Competency-Based Education" for the American Society for Training and Development in 1976, "Helping: A Growing Dimension of Management" for CRM/McGraw-Hill Films in 1980, "Working with the Adult Learner" for the Central Education Network in 1984, and a one-day workshop, "Understanding the Adult Learner," for Gulf Publishing Company in 1985. All of these programs included viewers' guides suggesting preparatory and follow-up activities. Clearly, I had become an advocate for the use of electronic media to involve people in learning.

Finally, the Computer Invasion

Starting sometime in 1978 or 1979 I had begun feeling increasingly archaic as more and more of my friends and colleagues were reporting to me how they were using computers in their personal and professional lives. I don't like feeling archaic; I like to think of myself as a frontiersman (remember, I grew up in Montana). So in October 1981, I got up the courage to announce to my wife that I would like a computer for Christmas. (After forty-six years of marriage, it becomes increasingly difficult to know what to give spouses for Christmas.) After thinking this over for several days she said, "OK, I'll give you a computer for Christmas; I'd like a mink coat," and we shook on the deal, thereby pretty well taking care of our savings account.

I visited several computer distributors, including Radio Shack (to look at its Tandy computer), Xerox, and Apple (IBM had not yet come out with its personal computer). After reading their brochures and watching several demonstrations, I decided on Apple—largely because it seemed to have a wider selection of software. On December 17 I went to the Apple distributor and bought the latest model, the Apple II+. As I began carrying the cartons containing the components up to my study, I became aware of the fact that I was salivating in anticipation of the joy I was going to experience with this new toy. I unpacked the components, set them up according to the diagram in the instructional manual, and then began reading "How to Get Started."

My first task, according to the manual, was to memorize about ten pages of commands and to practice each command on a game on the floppy disk that came with the package. I memorized about three pages of commands and practiced them on the silly game on the floppy disk, in which I had no interest at all. Then I had to leave to do a two-day workshop somewhere. When I got back, I raced up to my study, again full of anticipation. I turned the computer on and started retrieving the commands I had memorized a few days before. I think I got through about four commands (how to move the cursor up, down, left, and right) and went blank. After several days of trying again to memorize pages of commands and failing, I came down to the living room one evening and plopped myself into "my" chair, obviously dejected. My wife asked me what was wrong, and I said, "I have discovered that I am dumb; I can't even memorize the commands for using my computer." Her wifely response was, "Honey, you can't be really dumb; you have a Ph.D., and you don't get one of those if you're really dumb." It was then that I realized that it wasn't I who was dumb; it was the writer of the instructional manual, who just didn't understand that adults are task oriented in their learning and therefore wasn't helping me learn the commands I needed to know in order to get the computer to perform the tasks I wanted to accomplish.

I decided that I would have to teach myself and started by learning how to format a letter. I entered the commands that I thought would tell the computer to align the date line flush with the right margin and the name and address of the recipient flush with the left margin, to indent each paragraph five spaces, and similar instructions. Then I composed a letter, inserted a sheet of letterhead, and hit the "Print" key. What came out had the date line flush with the left margin, the name and address flush with the right margin, "Dear Joe" indented five spaces, and words in groups of three or four arranged more or less randomly down the rest of the page (I figured out later that I had occasionally hit the "Return" key instead of the space key). Clearly, I had entered the wrong commands, so I had to get out my instructional manual to find out what the right commands were. This was a real chore, since the manual of my word processing software (Apple Writer II) didn't even have an index. I had to start at the beginning of the manual and go through it each time until I came to the place where it dealt with the command I wanted.

After struggling with this self-didactic exercise for a couple of weeks I finally, toward the end of January, composed a letter that came out right. In another several weeks I had figured out how to compose my first article, with centered headings, underlinings, and footnotes. By early May I was so exasperated with the author of the instructional manual that I wrote a letter to Stephen Jobs, then chairman of Apple, describing my experience and urging him to get an adult educational consultant to come in and train his software producers and manual writers to gear their products to adult learners. (In the opening paragraph of the letter I explained that I was an adult educator—with a ten-page biography enclosed to document that fact—who was writing in the spirit of wanting to be helpful, not seeking a job; I even included the names and addresses of several adult educators in the California area who were available as consultants.) I emphasized the difference between "user-friendly" programs (a phrase used commonly in the computer industry) and "learner-friendly" programs.

I didn't hear from Jobs, but about six weeks later I got a phone call from Cupertino, California, from Apple's sales manager (think what this says about how computer people think). They were perceiving me as a dissatisfied customer, not as a potential helper. He asked me what the matter was, and when I told him about my experience, he said, "But, Dr. Knowles, you have to read the instructional manual." When I told him that I had read it until it was coming out of my ears and it still wasn't helping me, he said, "OK, I'll send one of our technicians from our Baltimore office down to tutor you." A few days later I got a call from the technician, and we made a date for him to fly down to Raleigh and spend a day with me. On the appointed day a young man (it seems that most computer experts are very young) appeared at my door and followed me up to my study. He opened the tutorial by asking what the matter was, and when I told him he also said, "But Dr. Knowles, you have to read the manual." I asked him to show me where in the manual a problem I hadn't been able to solve was dealt with, and he went through the same procedure I had so many times, starting on page 1 and reading until he found the answer on page 47. After a few more similar experiences, he exclaimed, "I see what you mean: the manual needs an index and needs to show you how to make the computer do what you want it to do. I'll pass the word along to Cupertino." My "tutorial session" ended before noon, and the technician departed. That was the last I heard from Apple, but I understand that its next model, the Macintosh, is much more "learner friendly."

I quickly learned, though, that the problem is not unique to Apple. In workshops during 1982 as I repeated this story to illustrate the point that adult learners are task oriented in their learning, I saw heads nodding all over the hall. When I asked the head nodders what make of computer they had, all computer companies were represented. Clearly, then, the problem was endemic to the industry.

This caused me to feel a deep sense of responsibility as an adult educator to do something about making the industry aware of its need to adjust its products and procedures to adult learners. I had a couple of weeks free in December, so I wrote an article for the *Training and Development Journal* in which I recounted my personal experience and that of many other computer users and made some specific recommendations as to what the industry should do to correct the situation. When I submitted the article the title I gave it was "The Computer Industry Needs Training—Now and Badly." I got a call a few days later from Pat Hurley, the journal editor, saying that it was a great article and that she would like to build the whole May 1983 issue around it; did I have any objections. I, of course, replied that I thought that was a great idea, since my primary purpose was to call the problem to the attention of the industry. When my May issue arrived, I quickly opened it to see what they had done to my article, and there it was in full—except that Pat had changed the title (and think what this says about the wonderful minds of editors). There, in large bold type, was the new title, "Malcolm Knowles Finds a Worm in His Apple." The next article was a report of an interview with an Apple representative. It was titled "Apple Responds—The Worm Is Turning," and in it, the representative explained that Apple was going to take my suggestions into account in developing its next model, the Macintosh. And, sure enough, it proved to be much more "learner friendly."

I take the space to describe this experience in such detail because it seems to document a fundamental problem that has caused the computer technology to be much less useful as a vehicle for delivering educational services than it is capable of being. The source of the problem, as I see it, is that the industry is dominated by engineers—people who understand the technical aspects of computers and can explain them to other engineers but who have very little understanding of how adults learn and how their technology can be geared to their unique learning processes, much less explained to them. There is still much room for progress, and I hope that adult educators will be more assertive than they have been in the past in promoting and helping in that progress.

Networking with Learners

My most recent experience with computer technology has been in using it for networking. I am a mentor for the Fielding Institute, an external graduate degree program in human and organizational development that is headquartered in Santa Barbara, California, but that has students scattered all over the continent. By means of a modem on my computer I am able to connect with students from Alaska to Florida through the Fielding Electronic Network and to dialogue with them about developing and executing their learning contracts, formulating their dissertation proposals, assessing the evidence of accomplishment of their contracts, and conducting their dissertation research. It saves me—and them—a tremendous amount of time. I can leave a message for them at any time of day or night, and they can respond at any time of day or night, and vice versa. We can even chat about our families, politics, and the weather—individually or in groups—as we would if we were meeting face-to-face.

I have done some reading about new developments in the use of computers for exploiting the concept of artificial intelligence, but I haven't yet had any personal experience with this new frontier, so I can only express the hope that it will open up another new world of learning resources. It is on my agenda for future exploration.

Some Projections into the Future

As I see it, we are just discovering that there are two keys to using these media for educational purposes: (1) interaction and (2) the human touch. Learning is a process of interaction between learners and their environments, including their experience and life situations. And there are two ways of providing interaction: providing opportunities for learners to interact with the program itself (by inviting them to make choices and then giving them feedback about the consequences of their choices and offering new choices), and providing for two or more learners to interact with one another and then with the program. A human touch can be maintained by having the program visibly involve real people as mentors and resource people so that the learners are not just facing a green screen but are looking at and relating to real human beings with real names and experiential backgrounds.

I am now convinced that most educational services will be delivered electronically within another couple of decades. Almost all American citizens already have television sets, and I am sure that through them they will have access to an increasingly rich variety of learning experiences, both informal and formal, that are congruent with the andragogical model. I feel certain that most citizens, of all ages, will have ready access to computers—in their homes and workplaces, but also in libraries, shopping malls, neighborhood centers, and elsewhere—that will connect them with fellow learners, resource persons, and interactive learning programs of all sorts. It is probable that without ever leaving home individuals can earn some college and graduate degrees in subjects that do not involve heavy equipment.

My friends in the biological sciences assure me that some of the major breakthroughs in our understanding of learning will come via the biological sciences, as more and more is discovered about what happens in the brain as we learn. Perhaps in the not-too-distant future we will have chemicals available to enhance memory, speed up the learning process, induce self-directedness, increase motivation, and heavens knows what else.

I think that the next several decades will be a time of the most ferment, innovation, and restructuring of educational systems in all of history. It will be an exciting—if sometimes a little painful—time to be alive.

I project what some of the implications of the technological revolution for the reorganization of our educational systems are in Chapter Eight.

Chapter 8

Looking Toward
the Twenty-First Century

How I Would Like to Be Educated
in the Twenty-First Century

Occasionally—especially on long plane trips when I'm tired of reading—I find myself fantasizing what it would be like to be reincarnated as a child in the twenty-first century, say, in the year 2025. More specifically, I fantasize about what would be required for me to be an "educated person" in that world and what kind of education would produce that kind of person.

Responsible futurists (for example, Botkin, Elmandra, and Malitza, 1979; Faure and others, 1972; Naisbitt, 1982; Schön, 1971; and Toffler, 1970, 1980) have convinced me that we are indeed entering a period of radical transformation of our civilization. The dominant characteristic of the twenty-first century will be an accelerating pace of change, not only because of the technological revolution but because of an explosion in the quantity of new knowledge and how it is made accessible. We have learned to adjust to change—the Industrial Revolution marked an era of change. But it was gradual change—what Schön calls "stable" change. What is new, never before experienced by humanity, is an *accelerating pace* of change, one consequence of which is the quickening rate of obsolescence of human beings.

131

I think that this new condition requires a redefinition of the purpose of education and the meaning of the "educated person." The nineteenth-century definitions of these terms, under which we are still operating, extol the preeminent value of knowledge. The purpose of education, this definition holds, is primarily to transmit knowledge (with some nodding to skills, understandings, attitudes, and values). The "educated person," therefore, is a *knowledgeable* person. In my twenty-first century reincarnation I would want an educational system that would help me become a *competent* person, with my highest competence being that of continuous, self-directed, lifelong learning—the ability continuously to anticipate new conditions and to change in ways that would enable me to avoid becoming obsolete. And I would want the same thing for all the inhabitants of this planet.

Other implicit objectives of the nineteenth-century model of education include the production of competitive people (achieved through norm-referenced testing, grades, and sports), chauvinistically patriotic people, conformist people (creativity is often discouraged if not punished), and dependent people (teachers have full responsibility to decide what is to be learned, how it is to be learned, when it is to be learned, and if it has been learned; the learner's role is to receive the teacher's transmissions and to do what the teacher directs). In my twenty-first-century life I would want an educational system that would develop cooperative people who see themselves as global citizens, are highly creative, and are self-directed learners. Of course, I would want them to be knowledgeable, too—but expandingly, not statically, knowledgeable.

I would want my twenty-first-century education to take place not in schools and colleges, as we have known them in the past two centuries, but in a Lifelong Learning Resource System. An LLRS would be a consortium of all the learning resources in a community, including the following:

- Institutions: specialized educational institutions, religious institutions, health and social service agencies, governmental agencies, museums, and libraries

- Voluntary organizations: labor unions, consumer and producer cooperatives, civic and fraternal societies, agricultural organizations, youth organizations, political organizations, and professional societies
- Economic enterprises: business and industrial firms, farms, markets, and trade associations
- The media
- Episodic events: fairs, exhibits, trips, rituals, and anniversary celebrations
- Environmental resources: parks, reserves, zoos, forests, deserts, lakes, and streams
- People: elders, specialists, families, and neighborhoods

The LLRS would operate under policies and procedures established by a governing board composed of representatives of the participating institutions, organizations, economic enterprises, media, and various categories of learners. It would be managed by a professional staff especially trained in lifelong education theory and practice, systems theory, information theory, and collaborative administration. In each community there would be a main center in which would be located a data base that contains information about all the learning resources available to the community (an educational brokering center) and makes that information available to all members of the system, including individual learners. There would be satellite centers within walking distance of every citizen.

Here is how I would like the LLRS to work for me. I would enter the satellite center nearest my home, starting perhaps at age four or five and returning periodically for the rest of my life. My first experience would be having an assessment made of my level of learning ability—my current level of skill in planning and carrying out a self-directed learning project. Skill development exercises would be provided, for both individual and small-group work, to help me move to a higher level of ability in self-directed learning—regardless of age.

I would then be referred to an educational diagnostician. This person would have access to a set of models of the competencies for performing various life roles, such as the following:

- The role of *learner,* including competence in reading, writing, computing, anticipating the future, conceptualizing, imagining, inquiring, intuiting, aspiring, diagnosing learning/change needs, planning learning/change projects, locating and using material and human learning resources (including computerized data banks), giving and receiving help from peers and resource people, and evaluating learning/change progress
- The role of *unique self,* including competence in self-analyzing, sensing, goal building, objectifying, expressing, value clarifying, accepting self and others, and being authentic
- The role of *friend,* including competence in loving, listening, empathizing, collaborating, sharing, helping, giving constructive feedback, and being supportive
- The role of *global citizen,* including competence in caring, participating, leading, decision making, discussing, acting, having perspective (historical and cultural), consciousness-raising, and being able to understand appreciate, and relate to other cultures
- The role of *family member,* including competence in maintaining health, planning, managing, helping, sharing, buying, saving, loving, and taking responsibility
- The role of *worker,* including competence in career planning, continuing vocational and professional development, using technical skills, accepting supervision, giving supervision, getting along with people, cooperating, delegating, and managing
- The role of *leisure-time user,* including competence in discovering resources, appreciating the arts and humanities, performing, playing, relaxing, planning, and risking
- The role of a *cultural literate,* including competence in acquiring and retaining the changing foundation of knowledge and values, which are the engine of our culture

The educational diagnostician would help me determine which life role, at what level of performance, would be appropriate for my next stage of development. He or she would then engage me in a set of performance assessments to determine what knowledge, understandings, skills, attitudes, and values I would need to acquire in order to achieve the level of performance we had agreed on. Some of this assessment process would be in small group activity in conjunction with self-administered assessment modules. I would leave the diagnostician with a profile of diagnosed learning needs.

Next, I would be referred to an educational planning consultant. This person would have immediate access to the data bank of learning resources and would work with me (again, often in groups) in designing a learning plan that would specify (1) the learning objectives derived from the diagnosed learning needs, (2) the resources that I would utilize in accomplishing each objective, (3) perhaps a time frame for completing each objective, (4) the evidence to be collected to indicate the extent to which each objective has been accomplished, and (5) the means by which the evidence would be validated (preferably through some form of performance assessment rather than merely information recall).

I would then go to the learning resources specified in the learning plan, wherever they might be in the community, and carry out the plan.

Upon completion of the learning plan I would return to the LLRS center for a rediagnosis of learning needs and the development of a next-level learning plan. This process can best be described as a "spiral" of learning projects, in contrast to a linear curriculum. A three-year-old might start with the simplest competencies of the role of *friend,* then move to one of the competencies of the role of *citizen,* and then to one of the competencies of the role of *learner.* These roles might well be the focus for the next several years, with increasingly complex competencies for each role—particularly those of the role of *learner.* In early adolescence the emphasis would gradually shift to the roles of *unique self, citizen,* and *worker.* In the adult years the emphasis would be on the roles of *worker, citizen, family member, leisure-time user,* and *cultural literate.*

Notice that there are no "teachers" in this system. There are educational diagnosticians, educational planning consultants, and resource people (in addition, of course, to administrators, information processors, and coordinators). These are roles that require a very different set of skills, attitudes, and values from those of traditional classroom teachers, and so a process of retraining of teachers would be required to put the system into operation. The resource people would function most like teachers, in that they would be content specialists. But they would be working with proactive rather than reactive learners; thus, their content resources would be used quite differently from those of traditional teachers. All of the professional workers in this system would see themselves as facilitators of self-directing learners.

I feel certain that given this approach to education I would indeed be able to survive—even thrive—in a world characterized by an accelerating pace of change.

Implementing the Shift from Now to Then. At this point many readers are probably asking, "How could such a drastic reorganization of our national educational enterprise be accomplished, and could we afford it?" I believe that it will take perhaps a couple of decades, but that it could be accomplished, and with the willing collaboration of our present educational institutions.

The fact is that elements of the concept of a Lifelong Learning Resource System are already in place:

1. There is already a substantial and growing discontent with the present lock step elementary, secondary, and higher educational system, as witnessed by several reports of the Newman Commission, the Carnegie Foundation for the Advancement of Teaching, UNESCO Institute for Education, and others. There is a growing awareness that what Botkin, Elmandra, and Malitza (1979) call "maintenance learning" (the acquisition of fixed outlooks, methods, and rules for

dealing with known and recurring situations) is not functional in a world of accelerating change and must be replaced by "innovative learning" (p. 10). The cry for "back to (old) basics" is being replaced by a cry for "ahead to new basics." In other words, a readiness for change is surging in our society.

2. The idea of competency-based education has made great strides in the last decade, especially in occupational and professional education. Competency models for a number of occupations and professions already exist. It would not be difficult or expensive to create task forces of experts and citizens to develop models of competencies for the several roles for ascending levels of maturity described above.

3. Nascent versions of the Lifelong Learning Resource System are being piloted in several communities under the auspices of the Community Education Association in the United States, Challenge Education Associates in Canada, and UNESCO in other parts of the world. It would not be difficult to create a task force to analyze their experience and construct a plan for gradually reorganizing our national educational enterprise, including reorganizing our teacher-training institutions so as to develop facilitators of learning rather than didactic teachers.

One thing is clear to me: We cannot afford to enter the twenty-first century with an educational system that permits (and even encourages) learning to stop at any stage or age. We must have a system that is organized around the concept of learning as a lifelong process.

What It Takes to Be a Competent Educator of Adults

First, I must confess that I think that there is no such thing as "an educator of adults" in pure form. There are many kinds and degrees of adult educators. For example, I perceive myself to be at least three kinds. I was first of all a developer and administrator of adult educational programs in a government agency and the YMCA. Then I became an administrator of an adult educational association. Then I was a professor of adult education, with a bent toward theory building and writing adult educational materials. Now, in my retirement, I am essentially a trainer of adult educational practitioners. In all these roles I was also a facilitator of learning.

There are also a large number of people who are working part-time or full-time as teachers of adults. Most of these people consider their main occupation to be something other than adult education; they are accountants, lawyers, business managers, clergy, teachers of children and youth, home-makers, consultants, real estate operators, and people in a host of other occupations. Many of them are volunteers in their adult educational roles.

But almost every adult has some sort of responsibility for helping other people learn, whether it be spouses, neighbors, co-workers, or friends. As one of my colleagues says, "It is a given that adult educational processes are useful and important in virtually all aspects of a rapidly changing social and economic environment. Hence, the competencies of an adult educator are needed by literally millions of people who scarcely know that they are adult educators" (Ingalls, personal correspondence, August 20, 1988).

Exhibit 2 lists the competencies that I perceive to be relevant to performing an adult educational role. They are presented in the form of a self-diagnostic rating scale, which I use in my training events to help participants become aware of the competencies they most need to develop. The first set of competencies, those for performing the role of learning facilitator, I view to be core competencies required to some degree by all people seeking to help others learn. I am sure that other competencies will be added to the list as the knowledge base of the theory and practice of adult education continues to enlarge. In fact, I would add one right now: "The desire and willingness to help others grow and develop."

You might well be asking, "Where can I go to learn these competencies?" Some of them can be gained from the printed materials listed under the references at the end of this book. Many can be acquired at the conferences of professional associations, such as the American Association for Adult and Continuing Education and the American Society for Training and Development. In addition, over one hundred universities offer short courses, seminars, and workshops, as well as graduate degrees, in adult education. Information about these resources can be obtained from the American Association for Adult and Continuing Education, 1112 Sixteenth Street, N.W., Suite 420, Washington, D.C. 20036.

A Bright Future for Adult Educators

As I point out in Chapter One, I did not choose adult education as a career. I just fell into it because I was warm and available when an opening presented itself and I needed a job. But I thank my lucky stars for that day in 1935 when the U.S. State Department notified me that there were no current openings in the Foreign Service, for I feel certain that I have had a much more fulfilling career in adult education than I could have had as a minor diplomat.

I was lucky, too, in a way, that I entered a new field still in the process of becoming. Lack of training or experience was no obstacle, since everybody in it was starting more or less from scratch in finding one's way in it. More importantly, we were involved in influencing, if not determining, what it would become. As the preceding chapters document, I relished the experience—and even enjoyed the risks—of being part of building something new and significant. I feel both pride and humility in having participated in the development of what has become the largest (and, in my estimation, most important) segment of our national educational enterprise. And, I must confess, I feel more pride than humility.

In reviewing my career, as I have done in the preceding pages, I occasionally felt some guilt that I had not done more to guide the movement into taking a more active role in providing leadership in addressing societal issues. The adult education movement in this country has not exerted the influence on national policies that the movements in several other countries have accomplished. But the guilt quickly evaporated

Exhibit 2. Self-Diagnostic Rating Scale.

COMPETENCIES FOR THE ROLE OF ADULT EDUCATOR/TRAINER

Indicate on the six-point scale by each of the competencies listed below: (1) the *required* level for excellent performance of the role you are in now or are preparing for by placing an "R" (for required level) at the appropriate point; (2) the level of your present development of each competency, by placing a "P" (present level) at the appropriate point. For example, if your role is that of teacher, you probably would place the Rs for the competencies for the role of learning facilitator higher than you would for the competencies for the role of administrator. You will emerge with a profile of the gaps between where you are now and where you need to be in order to perform your role well.

This is how it would look:

As you go, you will notice questions left blank. These are for your own use in putting in other competencies.

I. As a learning facilitator

A. Regarding the conceptual and theoretical framework of adult learning:

	P					R
	0 Absent	1 Low (aware of it)	2	3 Moderate (conceptual understanding)	4	5 High (expert)
1. Ability to describe and apply modern concepts and research findings regarding the needs, interests, motivations, capacities, and developmental characteristics of adults as learners.	0	1	2	3	4	5
2. Ability to describe the differences in assumptions about youths and adults as learners and the implications of these differences for teaching.	0	1	2	3	4	5
3. Ability to assess the effects of forces impinging on learners from the larger environment (groups, organizations, cultures) and to manipulate them constructively.	0	1	2	3	4	5
4. Ability to describe the various theories of learning and assess their relevance to particular adult learning situations.	0	1	2	3	4	5

5. Ability to conceptualize and explain the role of teacher as a facilitator and resource person for self-directed learners.

    0 1 2 3 4 5

6.

    0 1 2 3 4 5

B. Regarding the designing and implementing of learning experiences:

1. Ability to describe the difference between a content plan and a process design.

    0 1 2 3 4 5

2. Ability to design learning experiences for accomplishing a variety of purposes that take into account individual differences among learners.

    0 1 2 3 4 5

3. Ability to engineer a physical and psychological climate of mutual respect, trust, openness, supportiveness, and safety.

    0 1 2 3 4 5

4. Ability to establish a warm, empathic, facilitative relationship with learners of all sorts.

    0 1 2 3 4 5

5. Ability to engage learners responsibly in self-diagnosis of needs for learning.

    0 1 2 3 4 5

6. Ability to engage learners in formulating objectives that are meaningful to them.

    0 1 2 3 4 5

7. Ability to involve learners in the planning, conducting, and evaluating of learning activities appropriately.

    0 1 2 3 4 5

C. Regarding helping learners become self-directing:

1. Ability to explain the conceptual difference between didactic instruction and self-directed learning.

    0 1 2 3 4 5

2. Ability to design and conduct one-hour, three-hour, one-day, and three-day learning experiences to develop the skills of self-directed learning.

    0 1 2 3 4 5

3. Ability to model the role of self-directed learning in your own behavior.

    0 1 2 3 4 5

4.

    0 1 2 3 4 5

Exhibit 2. Self-Diagnostic Rating Scale, Cont'd.

D. Regarding the selection of methods, techniques, and materials:

	0	1	2	3	4	5
1. Ability to describe the range of methods or formats for organizing learning experiences.	0	1	2	3	4	5
2. Ability to describe the range of techniques available for facilitating learning.	0	1	2	3	4	5
3. Ability to identify the range of materials available as resources for learning.	0	1	2	3	4	5
4. Ability to provide a rationale for selecting a particular method, technique, or material for achieving particular educational objectives.	0	1	2	3	4	5
5. Ability to evaluate various methods, techniques, and materials as to their effectiveness in achieving particular educational outcomes.	0	1	2	3	4	5
6. Ability to develop and manage procedures for the construction of models of competency.	0	1	2	3	4	5
7. Ability to construct and use tools and procedures for assessing competency-development needs.	0	1	2	3	4	5
8. Ability to use a wide variety of presentation methods effectively.	0	1	2	3	4	5
9. Ability to use a wide variety of experiential and simulation methods effectively.	0	1	2	3	4	5
10. Ability to use audience-participation methods effectively.	0	1	2	3	4	5
11. Ability to use group dynamics and small group discussion techniques effectively.	0	1	2	3	4	5
12. Ability to invent new techniques to fit new situations.	0	1	2	3	4	5
13. Ability to evaluate learning outcomes and processes and to select or construct appropriate instruments and procedures for this purpose.	0	1	2	3	4	5

14. Ability to confront new situations with confidence and a high tolerance for ambiguity.   0 1 2 3 4 5

15.   0 1 2 3 4 5

II. As a program developer

A. Regarding the planning process:

1. Ability to describe and implement the basic steps (e.g., climate setting, needs assessment, formulation of program objectives, program design, program execution, and evaluation) that undergird the planning process in adult education.   0 1 2 3 4 5

2. Ability to involve representatives of client systems appropriately in the planning process.   0 1 2 3 4 5

3. Ability to develop and use instruments and procedures for assessing the needs of individuals, organizations, and subpopulations in social systems.   0 1 2 3 4 5

4. Ability to use systems-analysis strategies in program planning.   0 1 2 3 4 5

5.   0 1 2 3 4 5

B. Regarding the designing and operating of programs:

1. Ability to construct a wide variety of program designs to meet the needs of various situations (basic skills training, developmental education, supervisory and management development, organizational development, etc.).   0 1 2 3 4 5

2. Ability to design programs with a creative variety of formats, activities, schedules, resources, and evaluative procedures.   0 1 2 3 4 5

Exhibit 2. Self-Diagnostic Rating Scale, Cont'd.

3. Ability to use needs assessments, census data, organizational records, surveys, etc., in adapting programs to specific needs and clienteles.

    0   1   2   3   4   5

4. Ability to use planning mechanisms, such as advisory councils, committees, task forces, etc., effectively.

    0   1   2   3   4   5

5. Ability to develop and carry out a plan for program evaluation that will satisfy the requirements of institutional accountability and provide for program improvement.

    0   1   2   3   4   5

6.

    0   1   2   3   4   5

III. As an administrator
A. Regarding organizational development and maintenance:

1. Ability to describe and apply theories and research findings about organizational behavior, management, and renewal.

    0   1   2   3   4   5

2. Ability to formulate a personal philosophy of administration and to adapt it to various organizational situations.

    0   1   2   3   4   5

3. Ability to formulate policies that clearly convey the definition of mission, social philosophy, educational commitment, etc., of an organization.

    0   1   2   3   4   5

4. Ability to evaluate organizational effectiveness and to guide its continuous self-renewal processes.

    0   1   2   3   4   5

5. Ability to plan effectively with and through others, sharing responsibilities and decision-making with them as appropriate.

    0   1   2   3   4   5

6. Ability to select, supervise, and provide for in-service education of personnel.

    0   1   2   3   4   5

7. Ability to evaluate staff performance.

    0   1   2   3   4   5

8. Ability to analyze and interpret legislation affecting adult education.

    0   1   2   3   4   5

	0	1	2	3	4	5
9. Ability to describe financial policies and practices in the field of adult education and to use them as guidelines for setting your own policies and practices.	0	1	2	3	4	5
10. Ability to perform the role of change agent vis à vis organizations and communities utilizing educational processes.	0	1	2	3	4	5
11.	0	1	2	3	4	5

B. Regarding program administration:

	0	1	2	3	4	5
1. Ability to design and operate programs within the framework of a limited budget.	0	1	2	3	4	5
2. Ability to make and monitor financial plans and procedures.	0	1	2	3	4	5
3. Ability to interpret modern approaches to adult education and training to policymakers convincingly.	0	1	2	3	4	5
4. Ability to design and use promotion, publicity, and public relations strategies appropriately and effectively.	0	1	2	3	4	5
5. Ability to prepare grant proposals and identify potential funding sources for them.	0	1	2	3	4	5
6. Ability to make use of consultants appropriately.	0	1	2	3	4	5
7. Ability and willingness to experiment with programmatic innovations and to assess their results objectively.	0	1	2	3	4	5
8.	0	1	2	3	4	5
9.	0	1	2	3	4	5
10.	0	1	2	3	4	5

Source: Knowles, 1980, pp. 256–261.

when I realized that I am just not good at political action. My strength lies in creating opportunities for helping individuals become more proficient practitioners. I kept hoping that others would take up the mantle of leadership in political action, and several have made useful contributions in this direction. But, as I see it, this is still a yawning gap in our field and a challenging opportunity for the next generation of adult educational leaders.

Does the fact that I take such satisfaction in having built a career in the early stages of the development of our field mean that opportunities for similar adventuresome careers in the future will be limited? Quite the opposite. I am convinced that the next several decades will be the most revolutionary, expansive, and innovative in our field in all of history. The reason is that I see several fundamental forces at work in the world as we approach the close of the twentieth century, forces that will require a reorganization of our whole educational system around the concept of lifelong learning, with adult education being at the apex of the system. I have alluded to some of these forces in previous chapters, but let me review them and add some more.

1. Certainly the most visible, measurable, and irreversible force is our changing demographics. Within my lifetime the industrial societies of the world have been transformed from essentially youth-centered to adult-centered cultures. Consider this startling statistic: in the first census in which age was tabulated, in 1820, the median age of all American citizens was 16. The median age crept up during the rest of the nineteenth and first half of the twentieth centuries, but it didn't reach 21 until some time in the 1950s. In the census of 1980 the median age was 30.8 years. And the projections indicate that some time in the late twenty-first century it will reach 50. We have become a society of older and older people, and similar trends are beginning to appear in the developing countries. Think of the implications of this trend for our economic system, with an older and older work force and an older and older body of consumers. Think of the implications for our political system, with older people having an increas-

ingly large vote as well as a need for expanding governmental services. But most of all, think of the implications for our educational system. By far the largest segment of our national student body will be adults. Some of these implications are explored in Chapter Four, but the bottom line is that adult education will simply have to keep expanding to serve the needs of this growing population for continuing education. That means, of course, that the cadre of professional adult educators will need to continue to expand.

2.   A second force, which is dealt with earlier in this chapter, is the accelerating pace of change. The most serious implication of this force is that people will become obsolescent vocationally, socially, and psychologically unless they engage in continuing learning. As we move from being an essentially industrial society to becoming an information society, the kinds of skills required to be effective workers are shifting drastically. Millions of workers will have to be retrained to be able to get or keep jobs. But the new skills they acquire will themselves become obsolete quickly, and thus workers will have to be continuously retrained. But not only work skills will become obsolete; social skills will, too. As our population becomes increasingly mobile, changing places of residence more and more frequently, the ability to establish close relationships with new people quickly becomes a basic requirement for social survival. Human relations skills thus join reading, writing, and arithmetic as one of the "basics" in the educational curriculum. And all of this means, of course, the replacement of a basic attitude of stability with an attitude of adaptability for psychological survival. Adult educators are thus faced with the challenge of helping people evolve into what Toffler (1980) calls a "third wave" of humanity. We will have to learn to be holistic educators.

3.   A third force, which is perhaps a specialized extension of the second, is the expanding body of knowledge we are gaining about the process of learning. Until the middle of this century educational psychologists focused their research almost exclusively on teaching, or, more accurately, on the reactions to teaching by animals (mostly rodents) and young

children. The hypotheses of these psychologists were drawn mostly from the pedagogical model, in which control of the educational processes was almost exclusively the responsibility of the teacher. The researchers' primary goal was to discover how teachers could more effectively control learners, and the more teachers learned about control, the more controlling they became. As a result, our elementary, secondary, and higher educational system became highly control oriented.

It wasn't until the mid-1950s that we began to get substantial research on learning—on what goes on inside learners as they undertake to gain new knowledge, skills, attitudes, and values. This shift occurred as researchers began to investigate learning in adults and discovered that most adult learning takes place without the intervention of teachers. Houle's classic *The Inquiring Mind* (1961) and Tough's pioneering *Learning Without a Teacher* (1967) and *The Adult's Learning Projects* (1971) set the tone for this new line of inquiry. These studies led to a rising flood of research into the unique characteristics and processes of adults as learners, as cited in Chapter Four and other chapters, so that by the end of the 1980s we have accumulated a very respectable body of knowledge on this subject. Currently, research efforts are extending into promising new frontiers, including the physiology of learning, hemispheric differences (right brain, left brain) in learning, environmental influences on learning, the effects of extrasensory perception, and other aspects of learning. My prediction is that during the next decade the body of knowledge about learning (in children as well as adults) will at least double, and perhaps double again for decades ahead. So careers in adult education will surely require that adult educators be dedicated continuing learners. What an exciting thought—that our discipline is just now taking off to discover new galaxies in our educational space.

4. A fourth force, which is also an extension of the second, is the explosive development of educational technology. I describe this phenomenon in some detail in Chapter Seven, so let me simply repeat at this point my prediction

that within the next decade or two most educational services will be delivered electronically to learners, at their convenience in terms of time, place, and pace, and that learning programs will be highly individualized and interactive.

As a result of the effects of forces outlined above, I foresee a variety of new career tracks emerging in our field. These will be tied to the new roles that will be required to operate our national (and perhaps global) educational enterprise.

1. There will always be a need for the generalist, the person who has a broad understanding of the theories of learning, principles of designing a variety of learning experiences, methods and techniques of facilitating learning, the management of learning environments, and the principles and strategies of staff development—but who also possesses superb leadership abilities. I see this role as shifting from what we think of as administration (managing the logistics of operating courses, workshops, and the like) to the designing and management of systems of learning resources. I also foresee that these generalists will be managers of lifelong learning systems serving individuals throughout the life span. The institutional separation of childhood, adolescent, and adult education will largely disappear.

2. The largest number of adult educational specialists will be learning facilitators. These will be people who have a deep understanding of the learning processes revealed by the new research into learning and who will be highly skilled in helping individuals engage proactively in diagnosing their changing learning needs, designing and carrying out individualized learning projects, and evaluating their learning outcomes. This role will, by and large, replace the traditional role of teacher and, perhaps, the role of counselor.

3. There will need to be a variety of technical specialists, such as program designers, media and materials producers, specialized content experts, learning environment engineers, evaluation experts, and probably dozens of others not yet visualized. Much of the work of these specialists will be directly operational, but they will also be called upon to serve as consultants to the facilitators and generalists. They

must, therefore, be competent not only in their technical specialty but in performing the consultant role as well.

4.   The cadre of professors/researchers will have to expand exponentially to satisfy the growing demand for professional education, both preservice and in-service, and for a variety of types of researchers. My hunch is that this expanding aspect of our field will be given a new title, such as professional education in lifelong learning, and that it will be highly interdisciplinary and nontraditional in its policy and program structure.

As I see it, the one characteristic that will be shared by all these professionals in our field will be a deep dedication to the concept of lifelong learning and a sense of excitement about having a part in bringing about a "third wave" of humanity—people who value and excel in constant change.

I would love to be starting my career in this transforming era!

Articles by Malcolm S. Knowles:
A Chronological
and Annotated Listing

Len and Zeace Nadler, consulting editors for Jossey-Bass (and this book), wrote me on March 27, 1988: "The idea of listing all your articles is great! We would like to suggest an approach, however, that is much different from what is sometimes done. They should be listed chronologically, from the earliest to the most recent. For each, you should add a short note that could include comments relative to items such as these:

- why you wrote the article
- how your ideas have changed on that particular topic since it was published
- feedback from readers, either in writing or when you met them at some function or activity
- changes you would make if you were writing that article today

These would contribute to understanding *The Making of an Adult Educator.* Of course, some of that already appears in several of the essays, but it is not directly related to a time line of your articles that will show your insight, growth, and change." This suggestion struck a responsive chord in me, so here goes, with the articles numbered in the order in which they appeared.

While in High School

1. "How to Earn Fifty Merit Badges," *Boys' Life,* October 29, 1929. This was my first nationally published piece, and I think I wrote it because I wanted to share with other Boy Scouts a system I had worked out to enable them to earn the largest number of merit badges possible in a given length of time. It was also, of course, a sixteen-year-old's ego trip.

2. "A Memorial That Means Something," *Best Creative Work in American High Schools, 1929–1930,* National Honorary Society for High School Journalists, Des Moines, Iowa, 1930. I wrote this editorial for the Palm Beach, Florida, *High School News* and in it described how our senior class had decided to forgo publishing a yearbook and contribute the savings to alleviate the Depression-driven reduction in the high school's budget. I expect that my motivation was a combination of institutional pride and missionary zeal— persuading other high school senior classes to follow our example. In any case, it was awarded second prize for editorials that year.

While with the National Youth Administration

3. "This Job-Hunting System Works," *Your Life,* August 1939. I had been deputy director of the National Youth Administration for Massachusetts for four years when I wrote this article. One of my responsibilities was to develop a system for helping unemployed youth find jobs, and the system I developed (which was based on what at the time were fairly sophisticated marketing techniques) seemed to produce superior results. So my missionary instincts again motivated me to spread the word to other youth, and I chose as the instrument what was then the popular psychology periodical with the largest circulation. To my surprise, I received a check for $60;

in 1939 that was real wealth. And what a boost to the ego of an aspiring young writer!

While with the YMCA

4.   "Having Any Fun?" *Holiday*, September 1946. By 1946 I had been director of adult education at the Huntington Avenue YMCA in Boston for five years, with a heavy commitment to helping people make more constructive and satisfying use of their leisure time. I had picked up a number of ideas from the instructors of the Y's classes on how to find exciting hobbies. Also, I had been a navy lieutenant for a couple of years and following my basic training had quite a bit of leisure time on my hands. I decided that my most satisfying leisure time activity was writing, so I put together this article, passing along the wisdom I had picked up from the Y's instructors. I sent it off to *Holiday* magazine and was elated when it was accepted and I received a check for $100. Incidentally, the magazine carried perhaps a dozen letters in later editions describing how the article had enriched readers' lives. (Does one detect an incipient urge to be an adult educator so far?)

5.   "Adults Are Learning," *Crossroads* (Presbyterian Study and Program Magazine for Adults), October–December 1950. The editor of this new magazine asked me to give a broad overview of what was happening in regard to the education of adults in this country and where religious education fit into the picture. The article is fairly skimpy, and if I were rewriting it today, I'd be a lot more explicit and expansive.

6.   "Techniques of Constructive Controversy," *The Christian Register* (Unitarian), March 1951. In 1949 the Evanston Unitarian Fellowship, to which my wife and I belonged, became enmeshed in a series of controversies. I don't remember what they were about, but the minister was worried that his church was falling apart and asked me if I could somehow use the "magic" of group dynamics (which I was studying at the

time at the University of Chicago) to bring the church back together again. I agreed to try and asked that he call a congregational meeting in which all factions would be sure to be represented.

The first thing I did at the meeting was to split the congregation down the middle and form it into small groups of four or five. The groups on the left side I asked to list "things members do that we like" and those on the right side to list "things members do that we don't like." I asked one member of each group to report its list, and I wrote the items on sheets of newsprint, checking the number of times each item was reported. I had a helper tape the "we like" items on one wall and the "we don't like" items on the opposite wall. As I remember, the "don't like" list was somewhat the longer, and the item with the most checks was "making dogmatic statements," with the second most checked item being "monopolizing the discussion."

Then I had the members move around and form new groups of four or five and do two things: (1) list all the problems or issues they thought were causing controversy in the church, and (2) list all possible solutions to these problems or issues they could think of. I remember observing a group in which one member was obviously dominating and making dogmatic statements. After perhaps fifteen minutes she suddenly stopped, pointed to the "don't like" list, and said, "My gosh, I'm doing both one and two." Thereafter, she behaved as a constructive group member. As the reporters of these groups described their issues and possible solutions, I asked the minister to write these on newsprint sheets, combining similar items. During this process it became clear that most of the issues were quite superficial and seemed to disappear by virtue of simply being expressed. The few more substantial issues became the agenda for a series of task forces that were organized on the spot, with their reports being given at a later congregational meeting with similar results. It was clear to almost everybody that the church had changed from being an argumentative to being a problem-solving community after this experience.

Word about this event reached the editor of the *Christian Register*, and he asked me to write this article describing the process. Letters appeared in subsequent issues of the magazine for several years reporting similar experiences with the process. Suddenly I became the denomination's guru on group dynamics. In fact, I was asked to demonstrate the process at the Unitarian Universalist General Assembly in Hollywood, Florida, fifteen years later, in May 1986. I can't think of a thing I would change if I were to write the article today.

7. "A Farewell Message," *Adult Education News*, Chicago Adult Education Council, May 1951. My parting shot as the retiring president of the Chicago council, in which I boasted about progress made in the past four years and predicted a rosy future for the council (which turned out about the way many weather forecasts turn out).

While with the Adult Education Association of the U.S.A.

8. "Research in Group Dynamics Used in Founding the New Adult Education Association," *The Nation's Schools*, July 1951. A glowing account of how over two hundred delegates unanimously adopted a constitution for the new Adult Education Association of the U.S.A. in Columbus, Ohio, in 1951, using small-group processes under the expert leadership of Leland Bradford and Kenneth Benne. The punch line was "Mr. Robert, of Rules of Order fame, must have whirled in his grave at the way the meetings . . . were conducted."

9. "Antidotes for Dullness," *The Bethany Guide*, November 1951. An exhortation to use group dynamics techniques in religious education.

10. "Psychology, Religion, and Life," *St. Louis Unitarian*, January 1952. After making a case for a central tendency in social science research being the power of acceptance, understanding, and love in human relations, I closed with this modest challenge to religious institutions: "Think what it

would mean if human relations in general should become permeated with love rather than with fear, hate, suspicion, and distrust. Could it be that that the church has within itself the power to spawn the twentieth-century Renaissance in human relations? According to social science, the idea is far from fantastic." Looking at the strife around the world at the end of this century, I am not so sure that my challenge would be so modest if I were to write the article today.

11. "Move Over, Mr. Robert," *Adult Leadership,* June 1952. A diatribe against the divisive effects of the adversary spirit of parliamentary procedure and a plea to substitute problem-solving and consensus-building small group procedures. This stirred up quite a storm of protest among traditionalists and is one of the most-quoted articles I have written.

12. "Your Program Planning Tool Kit," *Adult Leadership,* June 1952. A set of guidelines for planning programs on the basis of the real needs of adult learners. Today I would place greater emphasis on gearing program designs and techniques more to the unique characteristics of adult learners, which we have learned about since 1952.

13. "Libraries and the Adult Education Association," *Public Libraries,* June 1952. Essentially an invitation (and plea) for librarians to take an active role in the newly formed AEA, of which I was now the administrative coordinator.

14. "Group Methods in Adult Education" (with L. P. Bradford), *Journal of Social Issues,* 1952, 7 (2). The central message of this article is summarized in the closing paragraph: "It is becoming clear that if we are to get a corps of adult educators adequate to the needs of the time we must add to their traditional training in subject matter content, educational methodology, and administrative skills, training in understanding the behavior of individuals, groups, and communities. The second half of this century requires social engineers and social inventors to bridge the gap between social science research

and action." I would repeat this message regarding the first half of the next century, unfortunately.

15. "The Role of the Librarian in Adult Education," *The Michigan Librarian,* December 1952. A plea for librarians to extend their roles to sponsoring more group types of activities.

16. "Adult Education—No Longer a Stepchild," *The Nation's Schools,* January 1953. Asked by the editor of this journal to give a "status report" and predictions for the future as the new administrator of the Adult Education Association of the U.S.A., I made a case for adult education's moving from a status of second-class citizenship in the national educational enterprise to a more central position. The punch line is "adult education is becoming big business."

17. "Mr. Douglas Goes to Washington," *Adult Leadership,* January 1953. An expression of hope that now that Paul Douglas was the new senator from Illinois, adult education would get more federal support.

18. "An Eyewitness Account of the International Conference of the Child in Home, School, and Community," *National Parent-Teacher,* February 1953. A highlighting of one of the themes of the conference: that the school can take a child who comes from a home in which nobody reads, writes, computes, or thinks only so far; that, therefore, the improvement of childhood education is essentially a responsibility of adult education. This is a theme I have repeated many times since 1953.

19. "Role Playing at Home," *Adult Leadership,* November 1954. A personal account of how my wife and I have used role playing to help our children (and their parents) better understand and accept another person's feelings and ideas.

20. "Role Playing at Home," *Presbyterian Survey,* May 1954. A reprint of article 19.

21. "How the Adult Education Association Works," *Adult Leadership,* April 1954. An explanation of the "participative management" philosophy and strategies of the new association, building on Article 8.

22. "What Does Social Science Offer to Association Management," *American Trade Association Executives Journal,* April 1954. Essentially an elaboration on the principles described in article 21 as applicable to other voluntary associations. I think I'd say just about the same things now.

23. "Communications Unlimited," *Adult Leadership,* June 1954. An explanation of the attempts being made by the AEA to facilitate communication among its members and between members and the association, including a primitive form of what now would be called networking.

24. "Education for Adults," *American Peoples' Encyclopedia Yearbook,* 1954, 1955, 1956, 1957. Contemporary views of the adult education movement.

25. "Recreation and Adult Education," *Recreation,* February 1955. Written at the invitation of the editor, its main point is that ideally there are some elements of both in each. I still believe this.

26. "Adult Education in the United States," *Adult Education,* Winter 1955. My periodic "state of the movement" message as executive director (note the change in title from administrative coordinator, which the executive committee decided confused people about who was in charge) of the Adult Education Association of the U.S.A.

27. "Adult Education," *Encyclopedia Americana,* 1955. A condensation of article 26, in which I proposed a definition of adult education that has been quoted a number of times since: "'Adult education' is used in three ways: to describe a

process, an activity, and a movement. Perhaps the most common usage is in reference to the *activity* of people learning together in groups. But people are increasingly recognizing that there is a *process* by which individuals can systematically learn from their daily experiences, and that this is also adult education. . . . A third meaning combines all the activities and processes into the idea of a popular *movement* that includes all the wide variety of mature individuals learning in infinite ways under innumerable auspices the many things that make life richer and more civilized. Those in the movement are dedicated to the improvement of the process of learning, the extension of opportunities for adults to learn, and the advancement of the general level of our culture."

28. "Deeds and Words in Adult Education," *Adult Education*, Spring 1956. An article I have lost and whose message I have no recollection of.

29. "A Report to Members on the 1955 AEA Delegate Assembly," *Adult Leadership*, February 1956. A summary of the policy decisions made by the AEA's governing body to strengthen the services and structure of the organization.

30. "Keep Your Discussion on the Track," *Methodist Adult Teacher*, August 1956. Some pointers from group dynamics for leaders in religious education.

31. "Learning by TV," *Adult Leadership*, October 1956. A much-quoted article, described in Chapter Seven, that attempts to apply principles of adult learning to enhance the educational impact of a then new medium. Today I would put more emphasis on providing for interaction between the learners and the medium.

32. "An Overview and History of the Field of Adult Education," *Adult Education*, Summer 1957. Another of my periodic "state of the movement" messages. Naturally, it shows great progress since the last one.

33. "Philosophical Issues That Confront Adult Educators," *Adult Education*, Summer 1957. A report on a national conference on philosophical issues called by Kenneth Benne, president of the AEA. Its main thrust is to document the wide variety of perceptions among leaders of the field about what philosophical issues are significant. A principal dichotomy arises between serving the needs of individuals and serving the needs of society, a debate that is still raging. My role was to do a balancing act.

34. "The Coming of Age of Adult Education in America," *National Catholic Education Association Bulletin*, August 1957. A plea for Catholic educators to see themselves as part of a larger movement that indeed is beginning to have some clout.

35. "Charting the Course of Adult Education in America's Future," *Adult Leadership*, October 1957. A working paper written at the request of Paul Sheats, chairman of the 1957 AEA national conference, to serve as a "thought starter" for discussions at the conference. The principal challenge I presented was how to prepare for accelerating change and expansion in the decade ahead.

36. "Direction-Finding Processes in the Adult Education Association," *Adult Education*, Autumn 1957. A review of the channels open to members to influence the direction of the AEA and a plea for them to get involved.

37. "Participation—A Golden Key to Learning," *Westminster Adult Leader* (Methodist), January-March 1958. Another set of proposals for the application of adult learning principles to religious adult education, the key being involvement of the learners in an active process of inquiry.

38. "AEA's Annual Report for 1957," *Adult Leadership*, May 1958. Another rosy picture of continued growth.

39. "What Should You Know About Adult Education?" *School Executive*, August 1958. A plea for the public schools to adapt their programs and methods to modern principles of adult learning.

40. "A Farewell Message," *Adult Leadership*, December 1958. An announcement of my decision to resign as executive director of the AEA after seven years and an expression of the gratitude I felt for the support I had received, along with a warm introduction of my successor, Glenn Jensen.

41. "Architecture for Adult Education" (with Herbert C. Hunsaker), *Adult Leadership*, February 1959. A report of the meeting of a national task force on the implications of principles of adult learning for the construction of facilities for adult education. The new Kellogg Center for Continuing Education at the University of Oklahoma is cited as the premier example of an attempt to translate these principles into brick and mortar, with an emphasis on multiple meeting rooms featuring oval seminar tables and comfortable chairs.

42. "Methods for Helping Adults Learn," *International Journal of Religious Education*, May 1959.

43. "Use Effective Methods with Adults," *Presbyterian Action*, August 1959.

44. "The Church Can Help Adults Learn," *The Church School* (Methodist), October 1959. Articles 42, 43, and 44 attest to my missionary zeal in trying to convert religious adult educators to the orthodoxy of participatory adult learning.

45. "The Effects of Community Influences on Adult Life," Chapter 6 in Lawrence C. Little (ed.), *The Future Course of Christian Adult Education*, University of Pittsburgh Press, 1959. Another plea for religious adult educators to gear their programs and strategies to the life situations of adult learners.

I am not sure why I had such a concern about religious adult education, except that I perceived that religious institutions constituted one of the richest resources in our society for the continuing education of adults and that on the whole they were using fairly traditional pedagogical approaches.

46. "Adult Education," *Social Work Yearbook,* 1960. An overview of the "state of the movement," with special attention to the role of social work in it.

47. "Understanding Ourselves as Adults," *Adult Leadership,* March 1960. A book review.

48. "What Should an Independent College Do About Adult Education?" *Wellesley Alumnae Magazine,* Fall 1960. Written at the request of the editor of my wife's alumnae magazine, this article proposes that every independent college has the responsibility to make its resources available for the continuing education of its graduates and the citizens of its community.

While at Boston University

49. "The New Graduate Program in Adult Education," *Boston University Graduate Journal,* February 1961. A description of plans for a new approach to graduate studies in adult education in which modern principles of adult learning would be applied so that students would experience them, not just hear about them.

50. *The Leader Looks at Self-Development* (pamphlet), Leadership Resources, Inc., Washington, D.C., 1961. A set of guidelines for continuing self-development by organizational leaders based on principles of adult learning.

51. "Leisure," *Westminster Dictionary of Christian Education,* 1962. A case for leisure's being an underutilized resource for continuing self-development.

52. "A Hard Look at Christian Adult Education," *Adult Leadership*, March 1962. A somewhat critical review of a book by that name by John Frye. I felt that Frye was largely ignoring what we now know about how adults learn and was criticizing religious education for the wrong reasons.

53. "The Role of Adult Education in the Public Schools," *Boston University Journal of Education*, April 1962. A review of the historical development of the role of public schools in the education of adults, an overview of their contemporary role, with predictions regarding their future role and some policy questions those predictions raise. I advocated a much more central role than, in fact, the schools have taken.

54. "A General Theory of the Doctorate in Education," *Adult Education*, Spring 1962. A plea for a consistent theoretical base for Ed.D. degrees, with the proposal that a "role theory" based on the development of competencies for performing the generalized role of "educator" as well as specified subroles, such as the role of teacher, administrator, counselor, and so on (and especially the role of adult educator), be seriously considered. This article has been widely cited and presumably has had some influence on graduate professional education.

55. "The Future of Adult Education," *School and Society*, September 1962. A reprint of Chapter 8 of my *The Adult Education Movement in the United States* (Holt, Rinehart & Winston, 1962) presenting (naturally) a rosy picture for the future of our movement.

56. "A Theory of Christian Adult Education Methodology," Chapter 5 in Lawrence C. Little (ed.), *Wider Horizons in Christian Adult Education*, University of Pittsburgh Press, 1962. A proposal for a coherent theory of religious education based on modern concepts of adult learning and geared to meeting both institutional and individual needs. In essence, it urges a shift from an "indoctrination" to an "inquiry" methodological emphasis.

57. "What Does Graduate Study in Adult Education Offer?" *Extension Service Review,* January 1963. A plea for agricultural extension workers to perceive their role as partly that of adult educator and to include adult educational courses in their graduate study.

58. "Adult Education," *Encyclopedia of Social Work,* 1963. An update of article 46.

59. "Adult Education," *Encyclopedia Americana,* 1964. An update of article 27.

60. "Group Methods in the Public Welfare Program," *Adult Leadership,* May 1964. A book review.

61. "What Do We Know About the Field of Adult Education," *Adult Education,* Winter 1964. A current view of "the state of the movement" documenting continuing expansion.

62. "Perspectives on Group Process," *Adult Education,* Autumn 1964. A book review.

63. "The Field of Operations in Adult Education," Chapter 3 in Jensen, Liveright, and Hallenbeck (eds.), *Adult Education: Outlines of an Emerging Field of University Study,* Adult Education Association, Washington, D.C., 1964. Another optimistic overview.

64. "Professional Education for Leaders of Continuing Education," *Boston University Journal of Education,* February 1965. An overview of the graduate programs in adult education offered in sixteen universities in the United States and one in Canada in 1964, with the observation that the demand for professional education in our field greatly exceeds this supply.

65. "Some Assumptions About Adult Learning," *Bulletin of Personnel Administration* (Girl Scouts of the U.S.A.), August 1965. An early presentation of what later became the andragogical model, with implications for training troop leaders.

66. "A Manual for Co-Leaders, The Adult Leader Training Course of the Great Books Foundation," *Adult Leadership,* November 1965. A review of the manual, with criticism of its leader-centered approach.

67. *The Leader Looks at the Learning Climate* (pamphlet), Leadership Resources, Inc., Washington, D.C., 1965. Some guidelines for establishing a climate conducive to learning.

68. "Adult Education," Chapter 9 in Rossi and Biddle (eds.), *The New Media and Education,* Aldine, 1966. Some beginning thoughts about how to incorporate adult learning principles into the use of electronic media. I have expanded my thoughts on this subject since then, as reported in Chapter Seven.

69. "The Role of the College and University in Providing Continuing Education from the Viewpoint of the College Administrator," *Nursing Education: Creative, Continuing, Experimental,* National League for Nursing, New York, 1966. A plea for an expanded role.

70. "Personal and Organizational Change Through Group Methods," *Adult Education,* Winter 1967. A laudatory review of the book by that title by Edgar Schein and Warren Bennis (Wiley, 1965).

71. "Program Planning for Adults as Learners," *Adult Education,* February 1967. A condensation of an address given at the 1966 annual conference of the Adult Education Association in which an updated version of the adult learning model and its implications for planning adult education programs were presented.

72. "Historical Development of the Adult Education Movement in the U.S.," a chapter in Rena Fory (ed.), *The World of Education: Readings,* Macmillan, 1968. Another of my periodic "state of the movement" messages.

73. "Working with Groups," *Adult Leadership*, March 1968. A review of a book by the same title.

74. "Andragogy, Not Pedagogy," *Adult Leadership*, April 1968. An adaptation of an address I gave upon accepting the Delbert Clark award at West Georgia College in 1967. It was the first full-blown presentation of my andragogical model of adult learning, which had been evolving for several years. At this time I perceived the andragogical and pedagogical models as being antithetical. As I explain in Chapter Four, I later came to see the two models as being parallel, with elements of each to be adopted or adapted to meet the requirements of particular learning situations. This article has been quoted extensively, and even fairly recently it has been cited in criticisms of my andragogical model—as if adult educators aren't supposed to keep learning, too.

75. "How Andragogy Works in Leadership Training in the Girl Scouts," *Adult Leadership*, October 1968. A description of the training program for troop leaders of the Girl Scouts, for which I served as the national consultant. As designed, the program was highly dependent on local Girl Scout councils being able to provide a local leadership training coordinator. As it worked out, the program was effective in those councils that were able to provide this service and flopped in those councils that weren't. From this experience I learned to have greater faith in self-directed learning.

76. "Andragogy, Not Pedagogy," *The Methodist Woman*, October 1968. A reprint of article 74 aimed at a specialized audience.

77. "An Experiment with Group Self-Directed Learning: The Learning-Teaching Team," Chapter 13 in P. Runkel, R. Harrison, and M. Runkel (eds.), *The Changing College Classroom*, Jossey-Bass, 1969. A description of my enhancement of participatory learning through the use of student teams that took responsibility for designing and conducting learning

experiences for the various units of graduate courses in adult education. This is a technique that worked so well that I have refined it and used it extensively ever since.

78. "Adult Education: New Dimensions and New Directions," *The Florida Adult Educator*, August–November 1969. A report of an address given at the Florida Adult Education Association challenging adult educators to break away from the pedagogical traditions of the past and provide services geared to unique characteristics of adults as learners and the unique needs of an information society.

79. "Gearing Continuing Education for the Seventies," *Journal of Continuing Education in Nursing*, May 1970. The central theme here is that with the rapidly accelerating change in medical technology, continuing professional education is the only way to avoid the rapid obsolescence of nurses.

80. "Adult Education," *Encyclopedia of Social Work*, 1970. An updating of article 58.

81. "The Handbooks in Perspective" (with Eugene DuBois), prologue to R. M. Smith, G. F. Aker, and J. R. Kidd (eds.), *Handbook of Adult Education in the United States*, Adult Education Association of the U.S.A., 1970. An analysis of the historical development of adult education as revealed in the series of handbooks beginning in 1934.

82. "Foreword," in J. Levin and F. Slavet, *Continuing Education: State Programs for the 1970s*, Heath, 1970. Applauding the precedent set by this pioneering overview of the adult educational leadership provided by a number of states and its challenge to other states to catch up.

83. "Seven Success Keys to Training Adults: The Modern Way," *Sales Meetings*, September 1970. An application of the andragogical model to sales training.

84. "Planificacion de Programs para Adultos Como Alumnos," Overseas Education Fund, Boston, 1971. The application of principles of program planning presented in article 71 to volunteer training in Latin America.

85. "Innovative Strategies for Continuing Education: An Overview," in *Report of the Eleventh Annual Training Institute for Psychiatrist-Teachers of Practicing Physicians,* Western Interstate Commission for Higher Education, Boulder, Colorado, June 1971. A transcript of a dialogic session on the application of the andragogical model to continuing medical education. A prominent theme in the issues raised was the resistance on the part of medical educators to turning over any control to the learners and ways to deal with this resistance.

86. "The Planning of Inservice Workshops," Southern Regional Education Board, Atlanta, Georgia, 1971. Suggestions for designing in-service workshops for teachers by having them first experience and then analyze the andragogical model.

87. "Andragogy, Not Pedagogy," in S. M. Grabowski (ed.), *Adult Learning and Instruction,* ERIC Clearinghouse on Adult Education, Syracuse, N.Y., 1971. A reprint of article 74 as part of a collection of articles.

88. "Professional Education for Adult Educators," *Journal of Continuing Education and Training,* May 1971. A restatement of article 49 for a different audience.

89. "A Systems Approach to Adult Education," *Newsletter,* Adult Education Association of Massachusetts, January 1972. My first attempt to apply systems theory to adult education enterprises, an approach that is greatly refined and expanded in later articles.

90. "The Relevance of Research for the Adult Education Teacher/Trainer," *Adult Leadership,* February 1972. A presentation given at the annual conference of the Adult Education

Association of the U.S.A. in Los Angeles in 1971 as part of a panel in which Paul Sheats gave a presentation called "The Relevance of Research for the University Adult Education Administrator" and Cyril Houle gave one called "The Relevance of Research to the Preparation of Professional Adult Educators." My approach was to trace the research contributions that had affected my practice as a teacher and to identify additional research contributions I felt were needed.

91. "Andragogy, Not Pedagogy," *Newsletter,* Department of Extramural Studies, The Chinese University of Hong Kong, May 1971. A reprint of article 74 for a different audience.

92. "Innovations in Teaching Styles and Approaches Based upon Adult Learning," *Journal of Education for Social Work,* Spring 1972. An application of the andragogical model to social work education, emphasizing the person-centered and developmental character of social work.

93. "Motivation in Volunteerism: Synopsis of a Theory," *Journal of Voluntary Action Research,* April 1972. A proposal for a theoretical framework based on Maslow's hierarchy of needs, in which motivation is geared to using voluntary service as a learning opportunity leading to self-actualization— rather than as just a duty.

94. "Ways of Learning: Reactive Versus Proactive," *Journal of Continuing Education and Training,* May 1972. A comparison of the difference in skills required for people to engage in teacher-directed reactive learning in contrast to self-directed proactive learning, with a plea for all of education to be concerned with developing the latter.

95. "Resume of Adult Education" (with Chester Klevins), in Chester Klevins (ed.), *Materials and Methods in Adult Education,* Klevins Publications, 1972. An overview of the state of the field of adult education to provide the setting for subsequent chapters.

96. "Foreword," in Elda S. Popiel (ed.), *Continuing Education in Nursing*, Mosby, 1972. An expression of appreciation for the publication of this book documenting the rapid growth in quantity and quality of continuing education in nursing.

97. "The Design of Education," *Journal of Higher Education*, Autumn 1972. Review of the book with that title by Cyril O. Houle (Jossey-Bass, 1972) extolling its virtues as a clear and scholarly exposition of the fundamental principles of program development in a variety of formats.

98. "The Manager as Educator," *Journal of Continuing Education and Training*, September 1972. Development of the proposition that an essential component of the role of a manager is the development of his or her employees, with some guidelines drawn from the andragogical model as to how a manager can provide an environment that is conducive to learning and can use strategies that facilitate human growth and development.

99. "An Approach to Consumer Education for Adults," Office of Consumer Affairs, Executive Office of the President, January 1973. A pamphlet to which I contributed a section proposing that everyday decisions faced by the consumer should be the starting points of learning experiences.

100. "Assumptions of Adult Learning: Andragogy, Not Pedagogy," *The Southern Baptist Educator*, June 1973. An adaptation of article 74, with special implications for religious education.

101. "Sequential Research Needs in Evolving Disciplines of Social Practice," *Adult Education*, Summer 1973. An attempt to provide guidelines (and justification) for shifts in the focus of research during sequential phases of development of a new discipline, such as adult education. I wrote this article in reaction to criticisms that research in adult education had been largely descriptive in its early stages, and I proposed

that in a new discipline the first need is to describe what it is. This has been one of the more frequently cited of my articles.

102. "The Process of Defining a Role in an Organization," *Journal of Continuing Education and Training,* Summer 1973. The abstract states that "People are hired to fill positions in organizations, but once in their positions they perform roles. They receive many signals from people both inside and outside the organization about how they should perform. The position-holder has at least seven options for dealing with these different and often conflicting signals. The most effective option may require some in-service education." Another plug for adult education!

103. "Issues in Adult Learning Psychology," *Prasar,* University of Rathjasthan, Jaipur, India, October 1973. A preview of article 110, for a different audience.

104. "Commentary on Mandatory Continuing Education for Professional Nurse Relicensure," *Journal of Nursing Administration,* November–December 1973. My main thesis was that society has a right to be assured that nurses keep up to date on the fast-changing technology of medical practice through mandatory continuing education, but that eventually the idea of continuing professional development will become so imbedded in the concept of being a professional that it will no longer need to be mandatory.

105. "Commentary on Entrepreneurial Achievement or Social Action by William Rivera," *International Review of Education,* December 1973. A review of Rivera's book in which I came out for a balance.

106. "Foreword" and Chapter 2 in Elda S. Popiel (ed.), *Nursing and the Process of Continuing Education,* Mosby, 1973. Applause for this book's promoting the gearing of continuing nursing education to modern principles of adult learning.

107. *The Use of Multimedia/Multisensory Approaches for Inservice Education* (pamphlet), ROCOM division of Hoffman LaRoche Company, 1973. Some more guidelines for using the media for interactive learning.

108. "Human Resources Development in Organization Development," *Public Administration Review,* March–April 1974. A plea for the perception of human resource development as the heart of organizational development.

109. "'The External Degree' by Cyril O. Houle and 'Diversity by Design' by Samuel Gould and others," *Journal of Higher Education,* March 1974. A review of two books that lay the foundation for and document the growth of nontraditional higher education. I proposed that both books are classics that will greatly influence the future development of higher education.

110. "Issues in Adult Learning Psychology," *Adult Leadership,* March 1974. Reproduction of a presentation at the Fiftieth Anniversary Symposium of the Division of Continuing Education of the State University of New York, Buffalo, October 15, 1973, in which I proposed that the most critical issues as of that time were (1) What is the purpose of education? (2) What is learning? (3) How do human beings grow and develop naturally? (4) How do adults learn?

While at North Carolina State University

111. "Lifelong Education and the School Curriculum," *International Review of Education,* Winter 1974. A review of a monograph with that title by R. H. Dave (UNESCO Institute for Education, Hamburg, Germany, 1973) in which I applauded UNESCO's leadership in conceptualizing the reorganization of schooling around the concept of lifelong learning.

112. "Nontraditional Study: Issues and Resolutions," *Adult Leadership,* February 1975. Reproduction of a presentation

made at the Adult Education Association conference in Miami in November 1974. In it I identified nine issues, some with resolutions: (1) What will we call it? (2) How will we define it? (3) How can public understanding of nontraditional study be gained? (4) What institutional changes will be required? (5) How will the curriculum be organized to provide articulation among levels? (6) How will learning be assessed? (By competency performance.) (7) How can students be converted from dependent to self-directed learners? (8) How can teachers be converted from transmitters of content to facilitators of self-directed learning? (9) What theoretical model will provide an integrated conceptual framework for a nontraditional study system?

113. "The Future Role of Libraries in Adult Education," *The Southeastern Librarian,* Winter 1975. My central proposition: librarians will serve as managers of electronic data bases and consultants to users.

114. "Adult Education: New Dimensions," *Educational Leadership,* November 1975. My theme: "The definition of adult education is gradually being changed to 'the art and science of helping maturing human being learn.' Since most adults are part-time learners, learning opportunities must be made available to them at times and places that are convenient to them and that provide easy entry and exit." This and other articles of this period give evidence of my deepening commitment to the concepts of nontraditional study, lifelong learning, and self-directed learning.

115. "Of Pedagogues and Andragogues," *Orbiter,* the Aerospace Corporation, 1975. An attempt to make the andragogical model relevant to engineers, as a result of a workshop I did for the corporation's training staff.

116. "The Manager as Educator," in James R. Lau, *Behavior in Organizations: An Experiential Approach,* Irwin, 1975. A reprint of article 98 for a different audience.

117. "Toward a Model of Lifelong Education," in R. H. Dave (ed.), *Reflections on Lifelong Education and the School,* Monograph no. 3, UNESCO Institute for Education, Hamburg, Germany, 1975. The skeleton of a model of a community educational system organized around the concept of lifelong learning—a model further developed later. Several articles around this period, including this one, give evidence of my growing interest in competency-based education.

118. "Concepts and Implications for the Necessity for Nontraditional Study," in R. J. Barak and R. S. McCannon (eds.), *Nontraditional Study: Threat, Promise, or Necessity,* Conferences on Nontraditional Study, Series 2, Drake University, Des Moines, Iowa, 1975. A presentation of some resolutions to some of the issues raised in article 112.

119. "Toward a Model of Lifelong Education with Special Reference to Midcareer Professionals," in F. Bottomly (ed.), *Peak Use of Peak Years,* Report of the 1975 Institute for Chief State School Officers, Georgia State University, 1976. An adaptation of the principles enunciated in article 117 to midcareer professional development, with special emphasis on networking.

120. "Program Development in Continuing Education," in P. K. Preus (ed.), *Marketing Continuing Education,* Memphis State University, 1976. Development of the thesis that success in marketing continuing education programs is directly related to the extent to which those programs are based on the real needs of individuals and their organizations.

121. "Last Gamble on Education: Dynamics of Adult Basic Education," *Adult Leadership,* February 1976. A review of a book with that title by Jack Mezirow and others (Adult Education Association, 1975), with special appreciation for its demonstration of the use of grounded theory as a research approach.

122. "Model for Assessing Continuing Education Needs for a Profession," *Newsletter,* Continuing Library Education Network and Exchange, March 1976. Proposal for a competency-based approach to assessing learning needs.

123. "Planning, Conducting, and Evaluating Workshops," *Training and Development Journal,* June 1976. A review of a book with the same title by L. N. Davis and Earl McCallon (Learning Concepts, 1974) applauding its congruence with the andragogical model.

124. "Separating the Amateurs from the Pros in Training," *Training and Development Journal,* September 1976. An observation that the professionals in the field understand and apply the modern concepts of adult learning whereas the amateurs tend to train the way they were taught.

125. "Four Keys to Better Staff Development," *Keynote,* the quarterly magazine of the Boys Clubs of America, September 1976. An application of the four key assumptions of the andragogical model to staff development.

126. "The Growth of Adult Secular Education and Its Thirty-Five-Year Development," *The Church School* (Methodist), October 1976. A report of an interview by Wayne Lindecker of the Methodist Board of Education tracing the growth of secular adult education in religious institutions.

127. "The Adult as a Consumer of Learning," in I. M. Newman (ed.), *Consumer Behavior in the Market Place,* Nebraska Center for Health Education, University of Nebraska, 1976. A review of the andragogical model (including contract learning) with its implications for gearing the marketing of adult education to the life situations and needs of adult learners.

128. "Lifelong and Self-Directed Learning," *Maryland,* University of Maryland, Winter 1977. A proposal that our

national educational system be organized around those two concepts.

129. "A Preceptor Program for Nurses' Clinical Orientation," *Journal of Nursing Administration,* March 1977. A proposal that clinical orientation be the major responsibility of andragogically oriented preceptors.

130. "Adult Learning Processes: Pedagogy and Andragogy," *Religious Education,* March/April 1977. An attempt to provide guidelines as to when andragogical and pedagogical strategies are appropriate in religious education, defending indoctrination as a goal in limited situations but proposing that an inquiry mode is more appropriate in most adult learning situations.

131. "The Leadership Passion: A Psychology of Ideology," *Adult Leadership,* May 1977. A review of a book with that title by D. Loye (Jossey-Bass, 1977). The review praises the insights provided about both the positive and negative consequences of an ideological approach to leadership.

132. "Adult Education," *Encyclopedia of Social Work,* 1977. An update of article 80 noting the continued expansion and professionalization of the field.

133. "The Adult Learner Is a Less Neglected Species," *Training,* August 1977. Report of an interview by the editors in which I document the growing body of knowledge about adults as learners.

134. "Andragogy: Adult Learning Theory in Perspective," *Community College Review,* Winter 1978. A tracing of the evolution of concepts about adults as learners from ancient times to the present, with the andragogical model as the contemporary capstone. Conclusion: "The field of adult education has long sought a glue to bind its diverse institutions, clienteles, and activities into some sense of unity; perhaps

andragogy will give it at least a unifying theory. And, extended in its application to the concept of lifelong education, perhaps andragogy will provide a unifying theme for all of education." After a decade of thought and experience I still harbor such hopes.

135. "People Don't Enjoy Being Taught," *The Train*, U.S. Civil Service Commission, Atlanta Regional Training Center, April 1978. Development of the thesis that adults may expect to be taught as dependent learners in a formal educational situation because of their previous conditioning in school but that their deep psychological need to be self-directing causes them to experience inner conflict and resistance.

136. "Adult Learning: New Strategies Needed," *Engineering Education*, May 1978. A review of the andragogical model, with suggestions as to its implications for new strategies in engineering education.

137. "The Learning Network: An Idea Whose Time Has Come," *NAPCAE Exchange*, National Association for Public School Continuing and Adult Education, Washington, D.C., May 1978. An exploration of the use of learning networks in public school adult education, with examples of its use in pioneering institutions.

138. "Continuing Education: The Role of the Professional Organization, A Theoretical Framework," *The Professional Medical Assistant*, May/June 1978. A report of my keynote address at the Invitational Conference on Continuing Education for Health Professional Organizations on March 9, 1978, in Chicago. The report contrasts traditional assumptions with "modern" assumptions about education and urges professional organizations to base their continuing professional educational programs on modern assumptions. Naturally, the modern assumptions include those of the andragogical model.

139. "Gearing Up for the Eighties," *Training and Development Journal*, July 1978. Two quotes are highlighted in the editor's introduction: "Trainers need to get on top of the concept and theory of competency development and to incorporate this system of thought into their philosophy of training" and "We should reconceptualize the role of trainer away from that of prescriber, transmitter, and evaluator of learning toward that of facilitator and resource person for self-directed learners." I also proposed a wider use of interactive electronic media for engaging members in continuing professional development. I urged training professionals to invest increasing energy in their own continuing professional development in order to avoid becoming obsolescent in the exploding technological revolution in training in the decade ahead, and I charged professional associations with having primary responsibility for providing the resources for this to happen.

140. "Converting Controversy into Creative Change," *Forum*, J. C. Penney Company, Fall/Winter 1978. An elaboration of article 6 for a different audience.

141. "Continuing Education: The Role of the Professional Organization," in *Proceedings, Invitational Conference on Continuing Education for Health Professional Organizations*, American Society of Allied Health Professions, Chicago, 1978. A reprint of Article 138.

142. "Needs Assessment Strategies and Techniques," in S. Gregory Bowes (ed.), *Distinguished Adult Educators Explore Issues/Trends/Strategies in Adult Continuing Education*, University of New Mexico, 1979. An elaboration of article 122.

143. "The Professional Organization as a Learning Community," *Training and Development Journal*, May 1979. A proposal that all professional organizations have a primary responsibility for the continuing professional development of their members and that they should therefore be conceptualized and operated as "learning communities."

While Retired

144. "Andragogy Revisited, Part II," *Adult Education*, Fall 1979. A response to the "andragogy debate" that had been carried on in this journal for several months. In the response I clarified some of my misinterpreted positions and modified some previous positions in the light of valid criticisms and subsequent research.

145. "How I Coped with Fads in Training," *Training and Development Journal*, September 1979. An observation that our field has a history of methodological fads, most of which I experimented with, adopting the ones that worked and dropping the ones that didn't.

146. "Retirement: Coping with Emotional Upheavals," *Lifelong Learning*, October 1979. A review of the book with that title by L. P. and M. I. Bradford (Nelson-Hall, 1979), with appreciation for its emphasis on maintaining open communications.

147. "The Fine Art of Educating Bosses," *Training and Development Journal*, October 1979. A description of techniques that colleagues told me they had used to expose their top executives to the new theories and methods of human resources development.

148. "A Little Historical Perspective, Please," *Training and Development Journal*, November 1979. An attempt to trace the historical development of human resources development in business and industry to help contemporary trainers to see themselves as part of an evolving field of social practice.

149. "Where Does Training Fit into the Adult Education Field?" *Training and Development Journal*, December 1979. An attempt to provide trainers with another perspective—as part of a larger adult education movement.

150. "The Growth and Development of Adult Education," in J. M. Peters and Associates, *Building an Effective Adult Education Enterprise,* Jossey-Bass, 1980. An updated historical perspective on the adult education movement, emphasizing the public's growing participation and support.

151. "Adult Learning: The Next Fifteen Years" (paper), the Learning Connection, Free University Network, Manhattan, Kansas, 1980. An optimistic forecast, with emphasis on the development of new delivery systems, particularly electronic.

152. "Preface," in J. L. Elias and Sharan Merriam, *Philosophical Foundations of Adult Education,* Krieger Publishing Company, 1980. An expression of gratitude for this important contribution to our philosophical literature.

153. "The Challenge of the Eighties," *Training and Development Journal,* January 1980. Report of the keynote address at the Fourth Annual Leadership Symposium of the American Society for Training and Development, August 1979. I outlined an early version of my conceptualization of an organization as a system of learning resources and held up the networking mode of the symposium as a model for training in the future.

154. "Some Thoughts About Environment and Learning: Educational Ecology, If You Like," *Training and Development Journal,* February 1980. An exploration of the positive and negative influences environmental factors exert on learning.

155. "Training as an Art Form," *Training and Development Journal,* March 1980. Development of the theme that the esthetic quality of a training event affects the quality of the learning it produces.

156. "What Do External Degrees Mean for the Training Profession?" *Training and Development Journal,* April 1980. An article extolling the virtues of the rapidly spreading exter-

nal degree programs in which trainers with full-time positions can pursue graduate study without extended residence requirements and class attendance.

157. "How Do You Get People to Be Self-Directed?" *Training and Development Journal,* May 1980. A description of techniques trainers can use to help people make the transition from being dependent learners to being self-directed learners, with emphasis on providing psychic support networks.

158. "The Magic of Contract Learning," *Training and Development Journal,* June 1980. Suggested guidelines for introducing and using learning contracts in training, with examples of its successful use.

159. "Lifelong Learning: Buzz Word or a New Way of Thinking About Education?" *Training and Development Journal,* July 1980. A review of the concepts presented in article 117, with the conclusion that this represents a new way of thinking about education.

160. "My Farewell Address: Andragogy—No Panacea, No Ideology," *Training and Development Journal,* August 1980. My final monthly column for this journal, in which I propound the thesis that andragogy is neither the model to end all models of learning nor a system of beliefs that demand blind adherence; rather it is a beginning framework of assumptions and principles to be tested and built on.

161. "State of the Art: Management Development—The Framework for Analysis," National Conference on Management Development in Health Care, the Wharton School, University of Pennsylvania, May 1980. An adaptation of article 160, with special application to management development.

162. *The Master Bibliography in Adult and Higher Education,* Nova University Center for Higher Education, Ft. Lauderdale, Florida, 1980. A comprehensive bibliography

organized by categories that has been widely distributed around the world.

163. "Foreword," in Bill Draves, *The Free University*, Follett, 1980. An enthusiastic endorsement of this first description of a new institutional form of adult education, which flourished temporarily and then receded.

164. "Foreword," in Eva Schindler-Rainman and Ronald Lippitt, *Building the Collaborative Community: Mobilizing Citizens for Action*, University of California, Riverside, 1980. Praise for the imaginative techniques pioneered by the authors for involving citizens in educative action projects.

165. "Andragogy," in Z. W. Collins (ed.), *Museums, Adults, and the Humanities*, American Association of Museums, Washington, D.C., 1981. A chapter applying the andragogical model to museum education and the humanities.

166. "The Future of Lifelong Learning," in Z. W. Collins (ed.), *Museums, Adults, and the Humanities*, American Association of Museums, 1981. Another chapter in same book as article 165; this chapter conceptualizes the role of museums in a lifelong learning community.

167. "Understanding the Adult Learner," *Proceedings, Southern Extension Marketing Workshop*, Nashville, Tennessee, April 1981. Development of the thesis that programs must be based on the real needs and unique characteristics of adults as learners if they are to be successfully marketed.

168. "The Day I Changed from Teacher to Facilitator of Learning," Follett *Educational Materials* catalogue, 1981. A description of my experience in converting a traditional undergraduate course at George Williams College into a student-directed process of academic inquiry. This short piece has been widely reproduced.

169. "Preface," in David Boud and others, *Developing Student Autonomy in Learning*, Nichols Publishing Company, 1981. An expression of gratitude to the contributors of this pioneering book for the contributions they have made to the implementation of the concept of self-directed learning.

170. "An Adult Educator's Reflections on Faith Development in the Adult Life Cycle," in Kenneth Stokes (ed.), *Faith Development in the Adult Life Cycle*, Sadlier, 1982. Development of the thesis that if the purpose of religious education in youth is to develop faith, the purpose in the adult years must be to deepen and enrich faith through self-directed inquiry.

171. "Modern Concepts of Adult Learning," *Data Processing Training*, Auerbach, 1982. A review of the andragogical model, with special application to data processing training.

172. "The Implications of Modern Concepts of Adult Learning for Data Processing Training," *Data Processing Training* (newsletter), Auerbach, 1982. A plea for data processing trainers to gear their training strategies to the real-life situations in which the learners are to perform.

173. "Self-Directed Contract Learning: Magical Inventions for Teachers of Adults," in *Proceedings, Conference on the Changing Student Population*, University of Wisconsin, Oshkosh, January 1982. More examples of the use of contract learning in traditional and nontraditional adult education programs.

174. "A Theory of Christian Adult Education Methodology," *Christian Adulthood: Catechetical Resources*, United States Catholic Conference, Washington, D.C., 1982. Some further thoughts on the application of the andragogical model to religious education.

175. "Foreword," in Neal Chalofsky and Carnie Ives Lincoln, *Up the HRD Ladder*, Addison-Wesley, 1983. An appreci-

ation for the creative way the authors have applied modern concepts of adult learning to the continuing education of human resources development professionals.

176. "How the Media Can Make It or Bust It in Education," *Media Adult Learning*, Kansas State University, Spring 1983. The application of the andragogical and pedagogical models to the use of media in education, thus "making it" or "busting it."

177. "Creating Lifelong Learning Communities" (working paper), UNESCO Institute for Education, Hamburg, Germany, 1983. A model for converting traditional educational institutions into elements in a system of learning resources making use of all providers of educational services in a community. This paper has been widely quoted around the world and is summarized in Chapter Eight.

178. "Adults Are Not Grown Up Children as Learners," *The Community Services Catalyst*, Fall 1983. A plea for the application of modern concepts of adult learning to all community education activities.

179. "Adult Learning: Theory and Practice," in Leonard Nadler (ed.), *Handbook of Human Resources Development*, Wiley, 1983. An update of my thinking about the andragogical model, with special focus on its application to human resources development in industry.

180. "Developing the Training Professional," in *Training and Development in Australia*, Carlton, Victoria, Australia, March 1983. A summary of principles developed in a series of workshops for the Australian Association for Training and Development, with special attention to the conditions unique to Australia.

181. "Malcolm Knowles Finds a Worm in His Apple," *Training and Development Journal*, May 1983. A description of my

traumatic experiences in trying to learn how to use my new Apple II+ computer for simple word processing by following the instructional manual. The title of the article when I submitted it to the editor was "The Computer Industry Needs Training—Now and Badly," because its main thesis was that the program developers and manual writers understood how the computer worked but not how adults learn.

182. "Making Things Happen by Releasing the Energy of Others," *Journal of Management Development,* University of Queensland, Australia, August 1983. This article is so foundational to my basic belief system that an adaptation of it is presented in Chapter Two.

183. "Lifelong Learning: A Passing Fad or a New Way of Thinking About Education?" a chapter in the *International Encyclopedia of Education,* 1983. An adaptation of article 159 for a different audience.

184. "Past, Present, and Future," *CEU Reporter,* May 1984. Excerpts from the keynote address at the Wingspread Conference of the Council on the Continuing Education Unit. In the address I traced the evolution of the concept of nontraditional study and predicted its growing influence.

185. "A New Role for HRD: Managing a System of Learning Resources," *Training and Development Journal,* May 1984. An elaboration on my evolving conceptualization of the application of systems theory to human resources development, with the HRD role shifting from managing the logistics of conducting training activities to managing a system of learning resources.

186. "Foreword," in E. J. Boone, *Developing Programs in Adult Education,* Prentice-Hall, 1985. An appreciation of Boone's "conceptual approach" to program development as a valuable component of the total process of program development.

187. "Shifting to an HRD Systems Approach," *Training and Development Journal*, May 1985. Some guidelines for facilitating the transition described in article 185.

188. "Interviewing an Expert in the Field You Want to Master," *Challenger*, May 1985. Some tips to self-directed learners on how to use experts as resources for learning.

189. "Older Adults as Learners," *Perspective on Aging*, the National Council on Aging, January/February 1987. Suggestions for adapting the andragogical model to the special needs, interests, and abilities of older adults, with an emphasis on the value of continued learning in helping adults maintain a future orientation.

190. "Foreword," in Martha John, *Geragogy: A Theory for Teaching the Elderly*, Addison-Wesley, 1987. An appreciation to this former student for her contribution to the development of a coherent theory of the education of the elderly.

191. "Adult Learning," Chapter 9 in Robert L. Craig (ed.), *Training and Development Handbook*, 3rd ed., McGraw-Hill, 1987. An updated version of the andragogical model, with special focus on its application to human resources development.

192. "Foreword," in David W. Stewart, *Adult Learning in America: Eduard Lindeman and His Agenda for Lifelong Education*, Krieger Publishing Company, 1987. An appreciation for this analysis of the contributions of one of the pioneers of the adult education movement, with an acknowledgment of my own debt to him.

193. "Enhancing HRD with Contract Learning," *Training and Development Journal*, March 1987. A further exploration of the use of learning contracts in human resources development, with more recent examples.

194.   "Knowles on Outside Resources and Adult Education,"
report of an interview with Jim Rapp, editor, *Sales and
Marketing Training*, April 1987. A plea for adult learners to
broaden their vistas regarding learning resources to include
all of the material and human resources in their environment.

195.   "Fifty Years of Training," report of an interview by the
editors, *Training News*, June 1987. An account of my perceptions of the changes that have taken place during my fifty
years of experience in the training field—most of them for
the better, of course.

196.   "Personal HRD Style Inventory: Are You an
Andragog?" Organization Design and Development, Inc.,
1987. A self-administered and self-scored instrument for
enabling individuals to place themselves on a scale from pedagogical to andragogical style.

197.   "What My Crystal Ball Says About the Future of Training," *Newsletter*, National Society of Pharmaceutical Trainers,
February 1988. A forecast of continued expansion and sophis-
tication, naturally.

References

Adams, J. T. *Frontiers of American Culture: A Study of Adult Education in a Democracy.* New York: Scribner's, 1944.

Adams-Webber, J. R. *Personal Construct Theory: Concepts and Application.* New York: Wiley-Interscience, 1979.

Apps, J. W. *The Adult Learner on Campus.* Chicago: Follett, 1981.

Arends, R. I., and Arends, J. H. *System Change Strategies in Educational Settings.* New York: Human Sciences Press, 1977.

Argyris, C. *Interpersonal Competence and Organizational Effectiveness.* Homewood, Ill.: Dorsey Press, 1962.

Baldridge, J. V., Curtis, D. V., Ecker, G., and Riley, G. L. *Policy Making and Effective Leadership: A National Study of Academic Management.* San Francisco: Jossey-Bass, 1978.

Baldridge, J. V., and Deal, T. E. (eds.). *Managing Change in Educational Organizations.* Berkeley, Calif.: McCutchan, 1975.

Baltes, P. *Life-Span Development and Behavior.* Vol. 1. New York: Academic Press, 1978.

Barron, F. *Creativity and Psychological Health.* New York: D. Van Nostrand, 1963.

Beals, R. A., and Brody, L. *The Literature of Adult Education.* New York: American Association for Adult Education, 1941.

Bell, C. R., and Nadler, L. *The Client-Consultant Handbook.* (Rev. ed.) Houston: Gulf Publishing Company, 1985.

Bennis, W. G. *Changing Organizations.* New York: McGraw-Hill, 1966.

Bennis, W. G., Benne, K., and Chin, R. *The Planning of Change.* New York: Holt, Rinehart & Winston, 1968.

Berte, N., (ed.). *Individualizing Education by Learning Contracts.* New Directions in Higher Education, no. 10. San Francisco: Jossey-Bass, 1975.

Blake, R. R., and Mouton, J. S. *Consultation.* Reading, Mass.: Addison-Wesley, 1976.

Boone, E. J., Shearon, R. W., White, E. E., and Associates. *Serving Personal and Community Needs Through Adult Education.* San Francisco: Jossey-Bass, 1980.

Botkin, J. W., Elmandra, M., and Malitza, M. *No Limits to Learning.* A Report to the Club of Rome. Elmsford, N.Y.: Pergamon Press, 1979.

Boyer, D. L. "Malcolm Knowles and Carl Rogers." *Lifelong Learning,* 1984, 7, 4.

Brookfield, S. D. *Understanding and Facilitating Adult Learning.* San Francisco: Jossey-Bass, 1986.

Bruner, J. S. *Toward a Theory of Instruction.* Cambridge, Mass.: Harvard University Press, 1966.

Bryson, L. *Adult Education.* New York: American Book Company, 1936.

Bullmer, K. *The Art of Empathy: A Manual for Improving Interpersonal Perception.* New York: Human Sciences Press, 1975.

Cantor, N. *Dynamics of Learning.* Buffalo: Foster & Stewart, 1946.

Carkhuff, R. R. *Helping and Human Relations: A Primer for Lay and Professional Helpers.* 2 vols. New York: Holt, Rinehart & Winston, 1969.

Cartwright, M. A. *Ten Years of Adult Education.* New York: Macmillan, 1935.

Chickering, A. W. *Education and Identity.* San Francisco: Jossey-Bass, 1969.

Coan, R. W. *The Optimal Personality: An Empirical and Theo-*

retical Analysis. New York: Columbia University Press, 1974.

Combs, A. W., Avila, D. L., and Purkey, W. W. *Helping Relationships: Basic Concepts for the Helping Professions.* (2nd ed.) Newton, Mass.: Allyn & Bacon, 1978.

Combs, A. W., and Snygg, D. *Individual Behavior.* New York: Harper & Row, 1959.

Cronbach, L. J., and Associates. *Toward Reform of Program Evaluation.* San Francisco: Jossey-Bass, 1980.

Cross, K. P. *Accent on Learning.* San Francisco: Jossey-Bass, 1976.

Cross, K. P. *Adults as Learners.* San Francisco: Jossey-Bass, 1981.

Csikszentmihalyi, M. *Beyond Boredom and Anxiety.* San Francisco: Jossey-Bass, 1975.

Darkenwald, G. G., and Merriam, S. B. *Adult Education: Foundations of Practice.* New York: Harper & Row, 1982.

Davis, G. A., and Scott, J. A. *Training Creative Thinking.* New York: Holt, Rinehart & Winston, 1971.

Deal, T. E., and Kennedy, A. A. *Corporate Cultures: The Rites and Rituals of Corporate Life.* Reading, Mass.: Addison-Wesley, 1982.

Dewey, J. *Experience and Education.* New York: Macmillan, 1947.

Dykes, A. R. *Faculty Participation in Academic Decision Making.* Washington, D.C.: American Council on Education, 1968.

Ely, M. L. *Adult Education in Action.* New York: American Book Company, 1936.

Erikson, E. H. *Childhood and Society.* New York: Norton, 1950.

Erikson, E. H. *Identity and the Life Cycle.* New York: International Universities Press, 1959.

Erikson, E. H. *Insight and Responsibility.* New York: Norton, 1964.

Erikson, E. H. *Dimensions of a New Identity.* New York: Norton, 1974.

Etzioni, A. *Complex Organizations.* New York: Free Press, 1961.

Fansler, T. *Creative Power Through Discussion.* New York: Harper & Row, 1950.

Faure, E., and others. *Learning to Be.* Paris: UNESCO, 1972.

Felker, D. W. *Building Positive Self-Concepts.* Minneapolis: Burgess, 1974.

Flesch, R. *The Art of Readable Writing.* New York: Harper & Row, 1949.

Freire, P. *Pedagogy of the Oppressed.* New York: Herder and Herder, 1970.

Gale, R. *The Psychology of Being Yourself.* Englewood Cliffs, N.J.: Prentice-Hall, 1974.

Gardner, J. *Self-Renewal: The Individual and the Innovative Society.* New York: Harper & Row, 1963.

Getzels, J. W., Lipham, J. M., and Campbell, R. F. *Educational Administration as a Social Process.* New York: Harper & Row, 1968.

Goldstein, K. M., and Blackman, S. *Cognitive Style: Five Approaches and Relevant Research.* New York: Wiley-Interscience, 1978.

Goodlad, J. I. *The Dynamics of Educational Change: Toward Responsive Schools.* New York: McGraw-Hill, 1975.

Goulet, L. R., and Baltes, P. *Life-Span Developmental Psychology.* New York: Academic Press, 1970.

Gowan, J. C., Demos, G. D., and Torrance, E. P. *Creativity: Its Educational Implications.* New York: Wiley, 1967.

Greiner, L. E. (ed.). *Organizational Change and Development.* Homewood, Ill.: Irwin, 1971.

Gross, R. *The Lifelong Learner.* New York: Simon & Schuster, 1977.

Gross, R. *Invitation to Lifelong Learning.* Chicago: Follett, 1982.

Guba, E. G., and Lincoln, Y. S. *Effective Evaluation: Improving the Usefulness of Evaluation Through Responsive and Naturalistic Approaches.* San Francisco: Jossey-Bass, 1981.

Gubrium, J. F., and Buckholdt, D. R. *Toward Maturity: The Social Processing of Human Development.* San Francisco: Jossey-Bass, 1977.

Havighurst, R. *Developmental Tasks and Education.* (2nd ed.) New York: McKay, 1970. (Originally published 1952.)

Hefferlin, J.B.L. *Dynamics of Academic Reform.* San Francisco: Jossey-Bass, 1969.

Herzberg, F. *Work and the Nature of Man.* Cleveland: World Publishing Company, 1966.

Herzberg, F., Mausner, B., and Snyderman, B. *The Motivation to Work.* New York: Wiley, 1959.

Hewitt, D., and Mather, K. *Adult Education: A Dynamic for Democracy.* East Norwalk, Conn.: Appleton-Century-Crofts, 1937.

Hilgard, E. R., and Bower, G. H. *Theories of Learning.* East Norwalk, Conn.: Appleton-Century-Crofts, 1948.

Hornstein, H. A. (ed.). *Social Intervention: A Behavioral Science Approach.* New York: Free Press, 1971.

Houle, C. O. *The Inquiring Mind.* Madison: University of Wisconsin Press, 1961.

Illich, I. *Deschooling Society.* New York: Harper & Row, 1970.

Ingalls, J. D. *Human Energy: The Critical Factor for Individuals and Organizations.* Reading, Mass.: Addison-Wesley, 1976.

Kagan, J., and Moss, H. A. *Birth to Maturity: A Study of Psychological Development.* New York: Wiley, 1962.

Keeton, M. T., and Associates. *Experiential Learning.* San Francisco: Jossey-Bass, 1976.

Kelly, D. G. *The Psychology of Personal Constructs.* New York: Norton, 1955.

Kempfer, H. H. *Adult Education.* New York: McGraw-Hill, 1955.

Kidd, J. R. *How Adults Learn.* (Rev. ed.) Chicago: Follett, 1973.

Knowles, M. S. *Informal Adult Education.* New York: Association Press, 1950.

Knowles, M. S. (ed.). *Handbook of Adult Education in the United States.* Chicago: Adult Education Association, 1960.

Knowles, M. S. "Androgogy, Not Pedagogy." *Adult Leadership,* Apr. 1968, pp. 350–386.

Knowles, M. S. *Self-Directed Learning: A Guide for Learners and Teachers.* New York: Cambridge Book Company, 1975.

Knowles, M. S. *The Adult Education Movement in the United States.* (Rev. ed.) Melbourne, Fla.: Krieger, 1977.

Knowles, M. S. *The Modern Practice of Adult Education.* (Rev. ed.) New York: Cambridge Book Company, 1980.

Knowles, M. S. "Malcolm Knowles Finds a Worm in His Apple." *Training and Development Journal,* May 1983, pp. 12–15.

Knowles, M. S. *The Adult Learner: A Neglected Species.* (Rev. ed.) Houston: Gulf Publishing Company, 1984.

Knowles, M. S. *Using Learning Contracts.* San Francisco: Jossey-Bass, 1986.

Knowles, M. S., and Knowles, H. F. *How to Develop Better Leaders.* New York: Association Press, 1955.

Knowles, M. S., and Knowles, H. F. *Introduction to Group Dynamics.* (Rev. ed.) New York: Cambridge Book Company, 1972.

Knowles, M. S., and Associates. *Andragogy in Action.* San Francisco: Jossey-Bass, 1984.

Knox, A. B. *Adult Development and Learning.* San Francisco: Jossey-Bass, 1977.

Knox, A. B. *Helping Adults Learn.* San Francisco: Jossey-Bass, 1986.

Laughary, J. W., and Ripley, T. M. *Helping Others Help Themselves: A Guide to Counseling Skills.* New York: McGraw-Hill, 1979.

Lefcourt, H. M. *Locus of Control: Current Trends in Theory and Research.* New York: Wiley, 1976.

Levinson, H., and Price, C. R. *Men, Management, and Mental Health.* Cambridge, Mass.: Harvard University Press, 1963.

Lewin, K. *Resolving Social Conflicts.* (G. W. Lewin, ed.). New York: Harper & Row, 1948.

Likert, R. *Human Organization: Its Management and Value.* New York: McGraw-Hill, 1967.

Lindeman, E. C. *The Meaning of Adult Education.* New York: New Republic, 1926.

Lippitt, G. *Organizational Renewal.* East Norwalk, Conn.: Appleton-Century-Crofts, 1969.

Lippitt, G. *Visualizing Change: Model Building and the Change Process.* New York: Wiley, 1978.

Lippitt, G., and Lippitt, R. *The Consulting Process in Action.* La Jolla, Calif.: University Associates, 1978.

Loevinger, J. *Ego Development: Conceptions and Theories.* San Francisco: Jossey-Bass, 1976.

McClelland, D. C. *Power: The Inner Experience.* New York: Wiley, 1975.

McGregor, D. *The Human Side of Enterprise.* New York: McGraw-Hill, 1960.

McGregor, D. *Leadership and Motivation.* Cambridge, Mass.: MIT Press, 1967.

McLagan, P. A. *Helping Others Learn: Designing Programs for Adults.* Reading, Mass.: Addison-Wesley, 1978.

Marrow, A. J., Bowers, D. G., and Seashore, S. E. *Management by Participation.* New York: Harper & Row, 1968.

Martorana, S. V., and Kuhns, E. *Managing Academic Change: Interactive Forces and Leadership in Higher Education.* San Francisco: Jossey-Bass, 1975.

Maslow, A. H. *Motivation and Personality.* (Rev. ed.) New York: Harper & Row, 1970.

Messick, S., and Associates. *Individuality in Learning.* San Francisco: Jossey-Bass, 1976.

Millett, J. D. *Decision Making and Administration in Higher Education.* Kent, Ohio: Kent State University Press, 1968.

Moustakas, C. *Finding Yourself, Finding Others.* Englewood Cliffs, N.J.: Prentice-Hall, 1974.

Nadler, L. *Developing Human Resources.* Houston: Gulf Publishing Company, 1970.

Nadler, L. *Designing Training Programs.* Reading. Mass.: Addison-Wesley, 1982.

Naisbitt, J. *Megatrends.* New York: Warner Books, 1982.

Overstreet, H. A. *The Mature Mind.* New York: Norton, 1949.

Patton, M. Q. *Utilization-Focused Evaluation.* Newbury Park, Calif.: Sage, 1978.

Patton, M. Q. *Qualitative Evaluation Methods.* Newbury Park, Calif.: Sage, 1980.

Patton, M. Q. *Creative Evaluation.* Newbury Park, Calif.: Sage, 1981.

Patton, M. Q. *Practical Evaluation.* Newbury Park, Calif.: Sage, 1982.

Penland, P. *Individual Self-Planned Learning in America.* Washington, D.C.: Office of Education, U.S. Department of Health, Education, and Welfare, 1977.

Pfeiffer, W. J., and Jones, J. E. *A Handbook of Structured Experiences for Human Relations Training.* 9 vols. San Diego: University Associates, 1969–.

Podeschi, R. L. "Andragogy: Proofs or Premises." *Lifelong Learning,* 1987, *11* (3), 14–16.

Poggeler, F. *Introduction into Andragogy: Basic Issues in Adult Education.* Privately published, 1957. (Cited by G. Van Enckevort in a paper presented to and subsequently published by the Dutch Centre for Adult Education, Amersfoort, The Netherlands, April 13, 1971.)

Pollack, O. *Human Behavior and the Helping Professions.* New York: Wiley, 1976.

Pressey, S. L., and Kuhlen, R. *Psychological Development Through the Life Span.* New York: Harper & Row, 1957.

Rogers, C. R. *Freedom to Learn.* Westerville, Ohio: Merrill, 1969.

Rogers, C. R. *A Way of Being.* Boston: Houghton Mifflin, 1980.

Rosenthal, R., and Jacobson, L. *Pygmalion in the Classroom.* New York: Holt, Rinehart & Winston, 1968.

Schein, E. *Process Consultation: Its Role in Organization Development.* Reading, Mass.: Addison-Wesley, 1969.

Schein, E., and Bennis, W. G. *Personal and Organizational Change Through Group Methods.* New York: Wiley, 1965.

Schlossberg, N. K., and Troll, L. *Perspectives on Counseling Adults: Issues and Skills.* Monterey, Calif.: Brooks/Cole, 1978.

Schön, D. A. *Beyond the Stable State.* New York: Norton, 1971.

Sheffield, A. D. *Creative Discussion.* New York: Association Press, 1936.

Simon, H. A. *Administrative Behavior.* New York: Macmillan, 1961.

Smith, R. M. *Learning How to Learn*. Chicago: Follett, 1982.

Tedeschi, J. T. (ed.). *The Social Influence Process*. Chicago: Aldine-Atherton, 1972.

Tennant, M. "An Evaluation of Knowles's Theory of Adult Learning." *International Journal of Lifelong Education*, 1986, *5* (2), 113.

Thorndike, E. L. *Adult Learning*. New York: Macmillan, 1928.

Tocqueville, A. de. *Democracy in America*. (P. Bradley, ed.) Vol. 2. New York: Knopf, 1954. (Originally published 1835.)

Toffler, A. *Future Shock*. New York: Bantam, 1970.

Toffler, A. *The Third Wave*. New York: Bantam, 1980.

Torshen, K. P. *The Mastery Approach to Competency-Based Education*. New York: Academic Press, 1977.

Tough, A. *Learning Without a Teacher*. Toronto: Institute for Studies in Education, 1967.

Tough, A. *The Adult's Learning Projects*. (Rev. ed.) Toronto: Institute for Studies in Education, 1979.

Tyler, L. *Individuality: Human Possibilities and Personal Choice in the Psychological Development of Men and Women*. San Francisco: Jossey-Bass, 1978.

Tyler, R. W. *Basic Principles of Curriculum and Instruction*. Chicago: University of Chicago Press, 1950.

Wlodkowski, R. J. *Enhancing Adult Motivation to Learn*. San Francisco: Jossey-Bass, 1985.

Zahn, J. C. *Creativity Research and Its Implications for Adult Education*. Syracuse, N.Y.: Library of Continuing Education, Syracuse University, 1966.

Zander, A. *Groups at Work: Unresolved Issues in the Study of Organizations*. San Francisco: Jossey-Bass, 1977.

Zurcher, L. A. *The Mutable Self: A Self-Concept for Social Change*. Newbury Park, Calif.: Sage, 1977.

Index

A

Academic standards, and adult learners, 19–20, 21
Adams, J. T., 12
Adams-Webber, J. R., 55
Adolphson, A., 28
Adult Education, 158, 159, 160, 163, 164, 165, 170, 179
Adult education: ancient roots of, 60–61; bibliographic reference on, 181–182; building support for, 86–89; in colonial period, 63; concepts of, 158–159, 173; and inequalities, 97; issues in, 86–100, 173; landmarks and heroes in, 60–72; literature on, 73–82; in middle ages and Renaissance, 61–62; modern development of, 62–72; in nineteenth century, 63–68; philosophical issues in, 160, 180; research on, 168–169, 170–171; status reports on, 157, 158, 159, 160, 162, 164, 165, 169; technology for, 117–130; time constraints in, 94; in twentieth century, 68–72; in twenty-first century, 131–150
Adult Education Association of Massachusetts, 168
Adult Education Association of the U.S.A. (AEA): and articles, 155–162, 167; conferences of, 165, 168–169, 173; Council of National Organizations of, 121–122; Knowles as executive director of, 14–16, 33, 77; as professional association, 70, 99–100
Adult Education News, 155
Adult educators: as administrators, 144–145; becoming, 1–24; competencies of, 137–139, 140–145; as facilitators of self-directed learning, 14, 21, 93–94, 140–143, 149, 182; future for, 139, 146–150; as generalists, 149; graduate programs for, 71, 139, 162, 163, 164, 168; heroes among, 60–72; insights for, 25–59; and institutional change, 95–96; new roles of, 149–150; and political action, 146; as professors/researchers, 150; as program developers, 143–144; selecting, 9–11; as technical specialists, 149–150
Adult Leadership, 79, 122, 156, 157, 158, 159, 160, 161, 162, 163, 164, 165, 166, 168, 172, 174, 176
Adult learners: networking with, 128; as self-directed, 89–94; workshops on, 39–45
Adult learning. *See* Learning theories

Boone, E. J., 20, 21, 81, 185
Boston: extension lectures in, 64; mechanics institute in, 65; National Youth Administration in, 7-9; settlement house in, 5; television series from, 122-123; YMCA in, 9-11, 33, 49, 73, 153; YWCA in, 29-30
Boston Center for Adult Education, 7
Boston University: and articles, 162-172; change by osmosis at, 95-96; Knowles as professor at, 16-20, 32, 33-34, 35; students from, 100, 108, 117, 123; theory building at, 45, 78, 79
Boston University Graduate Journal, 162
Boston University Journal of Education, 163, 164
Botkin, J. W., 131, 136-137
Bottomly, F., 174
Boud, D., 183
Bower, G. H., 46
Bowers, D. G., 53
Bowes, S. G., 178
Boy Scouts of America, Knowles as member of, 3-4, 5, 25-26, 152
Boyer, D. L., 98-99
Boys Clubs of America, 175
Boys' Life, 25-26, 152
Bradford, L. P., 15, 121, 156-157, 179
Bradford, M. I., 179
Brazil, workshops in, 32, 41-45
Brigham Young University, 108
Brody, J., 12
Brookfield, S. D., 81-82
Bruner, J. S., 79, 112
Bryson, L., 12, 71
Buber, M., 89-90
Buckholdt, D. R., 58
Bulletin of Personnel Administration, 164
Bullmer, K., 58

C

California, evaluations from, 108, 109

California, Davis, University of, evaluation from, 109
Cambridge Book Company, 32
Campbell, R. F., 53
Canada: community education resources in, 137; graduate program in, 164; and television series, 123; workshops in, 32
Cantor, N., 75
Carkhuff, R. R., 58
Carnegie, A., 66-67
Carnegie Corporation of New York, 70
Carnegie Foundation for the Advancement of Teaching, 136
Cartwright, M. A., 12, 70-71
Casey, E., 7
Catholic Church: and andragogy, 183; journal of, 160; and pedagogy, 62
Central Education Network, 123
CEU Reporter, 185
Challenge Education Associates (Canada), 137
Challenger, 186
Chalofsky, N., 183-184
Change: accelerating pace of, 131, 147, 160, 167; and creative leadership, 56-58; from evaluation, 112-113; institutional, 95-96
Chautauqua Institution, 65-66
Chautauqua Literary and Scientific Circle (C.L.S.C.), 66
Chicago: conference in, 177; Knowles family in, 12; YMCA work in, 30, 33, 49, 73
Chicago, University of: attitude at, 17-18, 33; courses at, 15, 32, 46, 49; extension department at, 66, 68; Houle at, 27, 60; Knowles as graduate student at, 12-14, 16, 30, 154; master's thesis at, 27-28, 75-76
Chicago Adult Education Council, 155
Chickering, A. W., 55
Chin, R., 53, 58
China, adult learners in ancient, 60, 61

204